# BRIGHT
# GREEN FUTURE

Dear Laura,

It was great to connect ad learn more about you work starting Sunrise in Little Rock. I have a lot of admiration for folks like you who do something transformational in areas that aren't particularly aligned ~~with the~~ politically. I'm excited for your next chapter in bringing climate education into the library.

I hope you enjoy the stories in BGF!

Best,
Trevor

TDC

# BRIGHT GREEN FUTURE

## HOW EVERYDAY HEROES ARE REIMAGINING THE WAY WE FEED, POWER, AND BUILD OUR WORLD

*by*

**GREGORY SCHWARTZ, PHD**

**TREVOR DECKER COHEN**

 **Harmon Street Press**
Berkeley, CA

**Bright Green Future**

Copyright © 2021 by Trevor Decker Cohen and Gregory Schwartz

ISBN 978-1506-910-34-5 PBK
ISBN 978-1506-900-18-6 EBK

LCCN 2021904537

First Edition April 2021

Cover art by Oručević Emir
Interior design by Olivier Darbonville

Published and Distributed by
First Edition Design Publishing, Inc.
In conjunction with Harmon Street Press
P.O. Box 17646, Sarasota, FL 34276-3217
www.firsteditiondesignpublishing.com

**Greg**

*For my sons,*
*Zion and Xander*


**Trevor**

*For my grandmothers,*
*Nana Jean and Gramma Joy*

# CONTENTS

## PART 4: FARMS • 111

## WHAT'S NEXT • 153

# Prologue

HUMAN BEINGS ARE REMARKABLY ADAPTABLE. IN A MATTER OF WEEKS following the outbreak of COVID-19, the entire planet was operating by a new set of rules. Societies around the world saw what needed to be done and we took massive, concerted action.

It hasn't been easy and the effects of this crisis will be felt for years to come. But our response to the pandemic shows us how rapidly we can pivot when we simply decide to do so. Now that we've been galvanized into action, there's another global crisis that needs our immediate attention—climate change and the degradation of the natural world.

This crisis can feel overwhelming. Too often, climate change ends up on the back burner, dismissed as too complicated or too burdensome to address. But as an Earth scientist for the past 30 years, I know it's well within our grasp to halt and even reverse the causes of climate change within the next few decades.

The solutions are already here. And now it's clear how quickly we can implement change as a global community. We're in a crisis, but it's also a huge opportunity to make long-overdue changes, and in many ways, emerge better than before.

This book is about the bright green future ahead and the people who are already making it a reality. We as the authors hope their stories inspire you, include you, and show you that we're already well on our way.

*Greg Schwartz*
*February 14, 2021*

# DOORWAY TO A BRIGHT GREEN FUTURE

———

'D JUST WALKED INTO THE LAST DAY OF A SOLD-OUT SOIL CONFERENCE. I was here to glimpse a quiet revolution of farmers and ranchers who were quite literally growing fertile ground out of thin air.

But before the talks began, and with a few minutes to spare, I made my way to the concessions table. It was here, as I helped myself to a cup of artisanal breakfast broth, that someone approached me from behind.

"Paper cups!" she said. "And we call ourselves eco-conscious here, but we're using paper cups. I don't see anyone with a reusable mug." She brandished a blue-rimmed glass.

In an attempt at sarcasm, I said, "Give me convenience, or give me death."

She turned to me and frowned. "You know, I've toured paper factories. They are horrible places. Chemicals and acids, streams that get ruined forever. Think about that as you use your paper cup, or any time you use paper. I always carry this glass. It's been in my family for 40 years and it serves me well. You need to think about what you're doing to the planet."

Ouch. I wanted to explain that I'd forgotten to pack a travel mug on my flight from California to Colorado, but thought I might be called out for not taking a horse-drawn carriage over the pass. I felt something familiar—shame. It was the shame that my everyday actions were destroying the planet. It was the shame that paper (not even plastic) cups weren't good enough.

The encounter reminded me why I was writing this book. It's an example of how ordinary people are often made out to be guilty for the destruction of the planet. We've somehow shifted the blame from polluters onto individuals. Meanwhile, the solutions we're given to remedy the massive problems in front of us are small actions, like remembering to bring our own personal cups to every event. These lifestyle changes are helpful. But there's a huge disconnect between the scale of small cups and the challenges of global waste and climate change.

Nick Tilsen, a Lakota activist and community builder, put it well. "The solutions to our problems have to be at least as big as the challenges that we're facing." As individuals, we're stuck with small actions, while shaming ourselves for massive, seemingly unrelated global challenges that are largely out of our control.

Into our cocktail of shame, we mix in a healthy dose of fear. Many of the messages we hear about the planet obsess over everything that's wrong. They project a nightmare future—all the hypothetical worlds we don't want for our children. They're very good at keeping us up at night, but not so good at moving us towards a solution. Fear may motivate us to respond to immediate danger, like the threat of a pandemic. But in the face of a slow-moving disaster like climate change, this emotion backfires. When everything may seem relatively fine on the surface, even if conditions are slowly getting worse, most of us learn to tune out or deny the constant cries of crisis.

For many years, before this project began, I'd sunk deeply into a combination of guilt and dread that could only be relieved by straight-up ignoring the problem. I'd been largely on the sidelines, trying to distract myself from the impending doom that kept popping into my news feed.

At the time, I was working for a vacation rental company, writing descriptions of seaside resorts, trying not to think that one day they may be under the sea. Maybe if I ignored it hard enough, climate change might somehow … not happen.

But then, something else happened. Through the magic dice of a Craigslist post, my partner, Lila, and I moved into an apartment with professor Gregory Schwartz. Though he was a generation ahead of me, he had more wide-eyed optimism than I ever did. It was a fearless and infectious optimism that mixed with a lifelong love for the planet.

One day, about a year into our time as roommates, I sat down on the couch. I was preparing to watch TV, but as I reached for the remote, I saw a manuscript on the coffee table. It was for a book Greg was writing about how to live more sustainably. I leafed through it, intrigued, not knowing what to expect. It wasn't the eco-friendly recommendations, but the shift in mindset that moved me. I'd been so caught up in the media of fear and shame that even a glimmer of hope had the force of a lightning strike. It blasted to pieces my doubt and doom, clearing a path for something new. When Greg walked in two hours later, I was still on the couch. I put the papers down. "I want to help you write this book."

This project began as an attempt to break free from the fear and shame that stifles us. It's a response to the idea that if we only focus on tragedy, if we only focus on all the things we don't want, then we'll never get a chance to work towards the world we deserve. Without that vision, the few with the power to forge our future will do it for us, and odds are, it won't be the one we want.

These words carried new weight in the wake of COVID-19 and the rising Movement for Black Lives. It often takes major crises to realize the urgency of creating a better world.

Greg and I had spent the last four years searching for stories that go beyond "How do we fix this mess?" and focus on "How do we make something better?" How can our human world live in harmony with nature? How can we create prosperity in our own backyard? What does the world we want to live in *actually* look like? Who's building it? And how can I be a part of that effort?

This book explores such questions through the stories of people working to answer them. These changemakers seek responses that are as big as the problems they face, but grounded in the places they love. It's a combination that melts through fear, shame, and inaction, and in doing so, reveals a blueprint for a better world.

# HUMAN—NATURE

—

BEFORE I MET TREVOR, I DID RESEARCH DEEP IN THE COSTA RICAN rainforest. Every morning I awoke to an alarm clock of howler monkeys, followed by a crescendo of bird calls and buzzing insects—radio signals in secret languages. A vaulted tree canopy created a three-dimensional space teeming with the density and diversity of inhabitants that you might expect in the skyscrapers of New York or Hong Kong. Remarkably, this natural metropolis had been there, in all of its complexity and abundance, for millions of years.

In this surreal setting, I was investigating how the human population was thriving because they were protecting, rather than exploiting, this ecosystem. I came to see that the beliefs and feelings that locals had about nature profoundly affected their actions toward it. Those who were raised to notice and appreciate nature—and especially those who deeply understood nature—were measurably more likely to protect it, both in their personal and professional lives. I believe this is true for all of us.

Ultimately, I was exploring a fundamental question about the relationship between people and the environment. How can human beings respect the timeless cycles of nature while still providing for our own needs? Even more importantly, what can we learn from those natural cycles about surviving and prospering on a rapidly changing planet?

We still have a long way to go towards acting on that learning. For every pristine swath of rainforest I've seen across four continents, I've witnessed another destroyed. I remember the sickly sweet aroma that filled the cabin on a bus ride in a densely forested section of Malaysia. You often smell it before you see it. Coming around a bend, I saw smoke rising off a charred clearing in the forest. Farther down the road, I saw the final result—a monotonous grid of palm oil trees.

An ancient forest had been replaced with a plantation that, with the aid of massive inputs of pesticides and fertilizers, would produce oil for a few decades. The irony is that palm oil was originally seen as a step in the right direction. The global food industry used it to replace trans-fats, while the European Union used it as a biofuel for cars in order to meet their carbon-reduction targets.

It seemed bizarre that a major solution to climate change somehow involved destroying the rainforest. It only made sense in an industrial system whose ethos had drifted far from the logic of nature. Natural eco-systems are highly adaptive and have shown, over hundreds of millions of years, how to replenish resources in infinite, iterative cycles. Though our human economy assumes that resources will never run out, it's de-signed to deplete them as quickly as possible. We take, we make, we trash. This kind of thinking may have worked when there were only a few hundred million people around, but not in today's crowded world. It's become clear that updating our beliefs and long-held assumptions is just as important as updating our technology.

If we want to save the planet, we have to think like the planet. All species on Earth are part of a circular flow of energy and resources. Hu-man civilization can and should start operating as *a part of* that flow, rather than *apart from* it. When we reimagine our economy like an eco-system capable of regenerating all of the resources it uses, we flip the script on our future. Instead of seeing fear and scarcity, we find oppor-tunity and abundance.

In writing this book, Trevor and I interviewed over 200 people who are building a future that heals the planet and enhances human prosperity at the same time. They're growing seeds of a new *regenerative* economy across four categories that account for essentially all the world's carbon emissions: energy, industry, cities, and farms. But these changemakers aren't just targeting carbon reductions. Their true aim is much bigger—a global renaissance.

They re-envision an *energy* economy that grows wealth for communities, emits nothing, and is organized around a symbiotic electrical grid. They reimagine *industry* as an ecosystem where materials replenish themselves. Steel, plastic, and concrete become nutrients in an urban environment that rebuilds itself, while unlocking millions of new jobs from the recovered value. In our *cities*, they show us how residents can use "tactical urbanism" to revive long-neglected main streets, and how dying malls can be reborn as walkable neighborhoods. On *farms*, they're creating a living infrastructure in the soil that becomes stronger with every harvest, reinvigorating and enriching farmers, while healing the land and ourselves.

Some people may think we need a great leader with a singular vision to master-plan these shifts. But agents of a better world are emerging from a million places. They're rising to the challenges we face at the local level, building small yet powerful parts of the larger whole. It's the same way that nature works, with different creatures forming communities in an ecosystem. This blueprint for change empowers us to create a vision for our own neighborhoods and cities, shaping our dreams for the next generation.

These concepts are not liberal or conservative. We offer no opinion on the merits of capitalism or socialism, or on whether the free market or the state is the righteous hand to seize the future. Nothing is supreme about either. Whether change happens through a government program, business venture, non-profit, cooperative, or some clever blend of them all makes no difference. What matters most is that these entities reflect the needs and desires of the people they serve.

This is a book about ordinary people doing incredible things. While they may be presented as intimidatingly smart or even a tad eccentric, they may also live right down the block. None of these individuals on their own have the power to move markets or draft era-defining legislation. But taken together, they can do much more. They can give the rest of us the power to create the world we want to live in. They make all of us the heroes of this story.

Where our own experiences as authors are relevant, we highlight who's narrating each chapter. In ones that don't mention either of us, we share the role of co-narrators. At the end of each chapter, you'll find questions that can help you explore the ideas discussed in these stories in your own life. This book is not a definitive guide of recommended steps to take, but rather, evidence of world-changing actions that are already happening. It's a gateway to begin imagining a new future in the places you care about most.

While we've selected specific stories, we don't mean to endorse specific people or organizations over others. Most of these stories are set in North America, and many of the solutions focus on people's experiences in these places. But there could be a book like this one written for every region on Earth.

For each individual featured, there are many more doing equally inspiring work around the world. In tales of injustice, it's often said that for every villain defeated, there are 100 others waiting to take their place. In this book, for every person trying to build a better world, there are 1,000 more already doing the same.

PART ONE

# Energy

———

"DON'T SEARCH, DIG, HOARD, AND FIGHT
FOR ENERGY. JUST PAUSE AND NOTICE
THE SUN WARMING YOUR SKIN AND THE
BREEZE BENDING THE TREES."

—ANONYMOUS

ABOUT TWO DECADES BEFORE MY TIME IN COSTA RICA, I FOUND MY-self on a trip in East Africa, walking through the savanna. After miles of open wilderness, I came upon a small home overflowing with people. Peering inside, I saw a crowd watching a soccer match on a television. But there wasn't a power line for miles. *How in the world do they have a TV out here?* I thought.

Then I noticed a modest, solitary solar panel on the roof. A few steps forward and I saw three more homes, each with panels and interior lights. I was amazed. If this remote, relatively impoverished village can be 100-percent solar-powered, then why can't we do the same in the United States?

The short answer is that it's possible for areas without electricity to entirely skip fossil fuels and go straight to renewables as they develop their economies. This is exactly what happened when much of Africa leapfrogged the expensive infrastructure needed for landlines and went straight to cell phones and cell towers.

In the US, however, modernization must confront the fossil-fuel industry. The conversion to renewables, while indeed happening, has been significantly slowed by the already entrenched energy sector and its broad influence.

An energy system has been created that is very good at two things: centralizing wealth and distributing danger. Most energy is delivered by utility monopolies or an oligarchy of oil. Protected from competition by the government and their sheer size, they have little incentive to modernize and can pass on the cost of not doing so to their customers and the general population. Yes, people can make a good living working for these enterprises, but ultimately they operate by sucking resources from a place until it's been exhausted and then moving on, leaving behind those they once supported. In every part of the system, from mining and burning to how the industry monopolizes markets and interacts with communities, the existing energy economy does little to respect the interests of ordinary people.

When South Carolina Gas & Electric spent $9 billion on a nuclear plant that was never completed, they raised rates, calling on their customers to pick up the tab. When power plant emissions lead to the deaths of 10,000 people every year in the US, our healthcare system absorbs the cost. When Pacific Gas & Electric went bankrupt due to negligence in the deadliest wildfire in California history, they got the taxpayers to bail them out. As energy expert and entrepreneur, Jigar Shah observed, "It's like all the upside profits I take and all the downside risks I socialize with the government."

The challenge we face is not just how do we switch to renewables, but how do we create a better energy system?

In this section, we show what that better system might look like. We go through many parts in the process, from the way energy is generated and distributed to how it's financed and how it's consumed. We see that change at any of these stages begins with a shift in mindset—the realization that it's possible to take back control over our energy production. We showcase how we might reverse-engineer the grid to create prosperity for the people and communities it serves. And we share the stories of next-generation energy providers, activists, citizen investors, and micro-grid savants working to build an energy future that respects and reflects the interests of everyday people.

# SYMBIOTIC GRID

---

I N A DECADE-LONG BUILDING BOOM OF RENEWABLE ENERGY, WE'VE reached a milestone. There are now one billion watts of wind and solar installed across the world. That's about half the capacity of all coal and three times that of all nuclear. To put *one* billion watts into perspective, at any given time, the entire Earth's population uses *eight* billion watts of electricity. Bloomberg's New Energy Finance estimated that while it took 50 years to reach the first billion, it will take just five years to reach the next, and it will happen at half the price.

But make no comparisons to the energy past. Unlike fossil fuels that produce a consistent supply of baseload electricity, renewables only generate power one-third to one-fifth of the time. The same logic no longer applies; the task is not to stoke an eternal flame with combustibles pulled from the deep. Our new goal is one of grace. Like Mother Nature, or a Zen master, we must find balance in the forces of night and day.

A new type of grid is needed to handle this balance. It's a symbiotic energy system that exchanges electricity, similar to how nutrients pulse through tree roots and food webs in a forest. Rather than the current one-way stream of electrons emanating from giant, isolated power plants, this new system will be composed of millions of interdependent sources of generation, storage, and adaptive response. While at first, this distributed network may be more challenging to manage, eventually it will enable a stronger grid that's less vulnerable to outages and provides dozens of mutual benefits to producers, consumers, and communities.

Clyde Louten is a maestro of this evolving modern grid, conducting the balance of renewables for the state of California. And while today he oversees one of the largest grids in the US, as a kid, he lived through daily outages.

"When I was growing up in the Caribbean, the picture on our 24-inch TV screen would shrink to about 19 inches or just disappear completely. The electricity supply wasn't consistent," he said. "Here in the US that would never happen—and if it does, there's practically a revolt."

At a young age, Clyde was the one in his neighborhood who knew how to fix the fuses when they wore out. He kept the lights on. Now he works to keep the lights on for the nearly 40 million people in the state of California. One day on the job, he got a call from his six-year-old daughter. The electricity had gone out while she was watching Nickelodeon. He laughed. "She calls and asks me to turn it back on."

He described his job as a balancing act that's "like walking on a razor's edge." It's a task that, in the past, was much easier. Before, with centralized energy sources that rarely vary, it was more straightforward to forecast the flow of electricity on the grid. Now, with tens of thousands of solar and wind farms with production varying with the forces of nature, it's become a challenging game.

He explained it like this to his daughter, who's now in high school: "Think about driving down a straight freeway at 60 miles per hour with your eyes closed. Every four seconds, you open your eyes to see where you're going. That used to be easy even five years ago, when baseload energy supply was so predictable. But now, it's not a straight highway and you're driving on a winding road of fluctuating supply. So every four seconds, you're quickly off track."

Over the course of one hour, Clyde said he's seen solar energy on the grid jump from zero to 7,500 megawatts. That's about a third of all the electricity that California uses coming online at once. Clyde referred to this as an "asynchronous grid," one that's based on power that switches on and off with the cycles of wind and sun. "We will eventually be very good at balancing it, but this transitional phase is challenging." A surge of too much electricity on the grid can destroy appliances. If there's too little current, time, as told by wall clocks, will actually slow down.

The variability of renewables is one of the fossil fuel industry's main arguments against solar and wind. It plays into our basic need for security and consistency. As such, the renewable grid requires a new mindset shift on energy management.

That's why Clyde conducted a test. He wanted to see if renewables could perform like traditional power plants. At a solar farm in the Mojave Desert, he and a team used advanced power controls to carefully regulate the electricity produced. In doing so, they found that solar could provide "spinning reserves, load-following, voltage support, ramping, frequency response, variability smoothing and frequency regulation," services usually provided by fossil-fuel plants. This low-cost breakthrough, along with others in scheduling solar generation, may allow us to bring a much larger percentage of renewables online. It could get us close to 30 to 50 percent solar on the grid, without even the need for batteries.

Energy storage is of course another pillar to balance our clean power future. Right now, when California produces more solar than its population uses, the state has to pay Arizona to take it. That oversupply can be captured in batteries and other storage systems. One innovative solution features giant water pipes nested in old mine shafts that use excess power to pump water up the shaft. When renewable production falls, the water is released to turn a turbine. Using gravity, we can store energy indefinitely to balance seasonal swings in renewable generation.

The need for energy storage may also work symbiotically with the rise of electric cars. During the workday, when most vehicles are parked, the noon sun creates more electricity than we use in our buildings. Those extra electrons can be saved in our car batteries and be put to use after work as we drive home on the sunshine.

When the sun sets, demand for electricity surges. A chorus of dishwashers, TVs, and appliances rises in the evening as solar generation drops off a cliff. It's during this peak that we may call upon our parked cars and their well-fed batteries to share some supply with a strained grid. They release their stored sunshine, lighting homes across a darkening horizon. As twilight fades to night, demand bottoms out. Prairie winds pick up, charging our cars as we dream. In the morning, we drive to work on the breeze.

This technology, in which electricity flows the other way from cars to grid, is known as "vehicle-to-grid" or V2G. It was largely theoretical for several decades. In 2018, pilot programs in the Netherlands, United Kingdom, and Germany have shown that it works. Importantly, the fears around battery degradation have been calmed by tests that show Tesla batteries can run for over 300,000 miles and still work at 85 percent capacity. Other studies reveal the yet untapped potential of V2G. It's estimated that one million electric vehicles with a range of 200 miles would be enough to back up the entire California grid with energy storage. There are currently 15 million vehicles in the state.

Beyond its benefits to the grid, V2G may fundamentally change the economics of car ownership. A pilot program in the UK led by the battery company Moixa paid Nissan Leaf owners up to $75 a month for discharging onto the grid. Over the course of the year, that may work out to $900. Every year, the average US household spends $9,000 on transportation. It's the second biggest expense after housing. Electric cars cost about one-third as much to maintain as do internal combustion cars, and the electricity that powers them is about half the price of gasoline per mile. When we combine these savings with payments from V2G, we may transform one of the biggest costs for families into a source of income.

For car companies, V2G may create an entirely new way to look at sales. "As a car-maker, it could be interesting to actually offer V2G as an option to your customer," said Marten Hamelink, a researcher for electric vehicles with the Dutch government. "In the future, you may have the cost of the car, but with incentives for using the battery on the grid and smart charging, you won't have to pay for *running* your car."

There are, of course, well-placed concerns that a boom in electric ve-hicles will spike demand for fossil-fuel power plants. Indeed, the current centralized grid treats every increase in load as a need to generate more power. In a symbiotic energy system, however, more electric cars may actually expand storage for wind and solar, evening out their variability. In addition, at the end of the battery's life, when it's no longer strong enough to power a car, it's still far from useless. It may find a second life as stationary storage on the grid. The electric bus company, Proterra, estimates that its vehicle batteries could last another ten years, providing back-up for the grid. Every electric car made today is potentially more storage to balance renewables tomorrow.

Managing the *supply* of energy isn't everything, though. *Demand* is a strong pillar in balancing the clean grid of the future. We can respond to critical times of high electricity usage and lessen the burden on the overall system. In programs known as "demand response," utilities pay businesses and homeowners to reduce electricity use on peak hours and days. Pool heaters, fridges, and air conditioners can be programmed to respond to fluctuations in power demand. Everything that's connected to the grid can work together as a decentralized network. As the oper-ators of those devices, we may earn money for helping to reduce strain on the overall system. Several major utility companies already offer dis-counts for participating in demand response.

As we sharpen our ability to store, manage, and use energy, the nature of the grid itself is changing. With solar panel systems that fit on a rooftop and batteries whose prices have fallen by 80 percent in five years, the need for a monumental grid may become obsolete. Places that have never had electricity before are skipping the need for centralized power plants entirely.

Nicole Poindexter runs Energicity, a company in West Africa that installs solar microgrids in rural villages. These are self-sustaining islands of electricity in a sea of energy poverty. Beyond powering LED lights in homes, which can replace expensive kerosene lanterns, Energicity's microgrids are strong enough to run light industry. Before they electrified the village of Odumasi, Ghana, one family was forced to separate. The mother moved to the city in order to use an electric sewing machine for her seamstress business. It's one story in a larger narrative of families adapting to a modernizing world. When Black Star Energy, the Ghanian subsidiary of Energicity, electrified her village, she could move her business back home. The family was reunited.

"Electricity doesn't just power lights and TVs, it transforms people's lives," said Nicole. For many in the rural, developing world, microgrids can be a pathway into a new standard of living. Moreover, electricity can save lives. At a nearby health clinic, the microgrid allowed for an ultrasound machine to check for complications in pregnancy. These improvements reduced deaths of mothers during childbirth.

The 15 villages that Nicole's business helped electrify have done something revolutionary. They've leapfrogged the need for a centralized grid based on fossil fuels. They jumped from no electricity to 100-percent clean power. Solar microgrids may become the first source of power for the nearly one billion people who still lack access to electricity.

Even as microgrids declare their independence from the system, that may not be an end in itself. For the microgrid can be a pillar to help balance the megagrid. An electrified village that generates its own power may encourage connections to the larger grid by a transmission line. These self-contained systems can help strengthen many developing-world grids prone to outages by producing or storing extra power as needed. In addition, the smart meters that enable payments on the microgrid can help reduce energy theft. Currently, many people find ways to siphon power from the wires above, which can be a drain on expanding electrification in the developing world.

In developed countries, microgrids make the overall system more resilient and can provide crucial emergency services. During the Sonoma, California wildfires that knocked out power for most residents, one solar microgrid provided consistent electricity for ten days. We don't have to rely solely on a top-heavy, centralized energy system that collapses when a few parts break. By nesting microgrids that can stand on their own, we deepen the resilience of the whole.

The transition to a grid powered by distributed renewables may be challenging at first. Ultimately, though it has the potential to create a better energy system and economy. With decentralized sources of electricity come decentralized benefits. No longer must all services be provided by a monolithic power authority. Everyone who participates has the opportunity to share in the wealth of the system. This way of thinking shatters what many dismissed as impossible. We *can* move to a fully renewable future, and we can do it guided by the leadership of ordinary people.

Some of the concepts in this chapter, like V2G, may be still in the pilot phase, but it's important to start asking for a system built on principles that favor people over power companies. We have an opportunity to create a new symbiotic grid balanced by relationships of mutual benefit between transportation and generation, energy supply and demand, microgrids and megagrids. When put at odds, these forces leave us with additional challenges. When brought together, they form electric harmonies, composed of empowered consumers and communities.

## KEEP EXPLORING

- *What might a symbiotic grid look like in my community, and how might I benefit and contribute to it?*

- *Are there vehicle-to-grid or demand response programs offered by my utility or other grid operators? If not, ask why not.*

# POWER TO GROW
# WEALTH FOR ALL

———

W E'RE AT THE EDGE OF A REVOLUTION THAT HIDES BEHIND THE meter. Unless the power goes out, it's easy not to think much about where the energy comes from and who controls it. Utilities and large investors have taken advantage of that fact, monopolizing profits from electricity, while passing on risks to ratepayers, taxpayers, and nearby residents.

In a bright energy future, the source of power grows wealth for those it serves. It's a future being created as we speak by an alliance of communities, workers, and investors in small towns and urban neighborhoods across the world. A better energy future is as much about switching to wind and solar as it is about changing the nature of the game.

On a road trip once, I came face-to-face with the renewable energy revolution. I was racing across the panhandle of Texas in the shadow of giants, following the same route Greg had made many times. The land was as flat as flat can be, the horizon not unlike the open ocean. In the past, when I'd driven through the Redwoods, I'd never quite gotten a sense for how tall they were. The branches made a crown and the trees seemed to drift off into infinity. But here in the treeless flatlands, I saw the giant turbine's naked power. I imagined a silver birch, super-sized beyond all recognition. Its three branches caught the wind, absorbing a timeless energy that whipped through the Great Plains, rocking my car from side to side. I tightened my grip on the wheel and focused back on the road.

The Great Plains are the Saudi Arabia of wind. From South Dakota to Texas, over 10,000 turbines generate enough electricity to power 14 million homes, or about 11 percent of all US households. Steve Sershen, whose company finances wind farms, calls it "God's flyway."

"The wind blows from north to south. Northern plains have the wind during the day. Southern plains have the wind at night." Capturing the forces of this vast, open range can provide consistent power when balanced over the whole.

Yet a lot of the wealth from these wind farms funnels into the deep pockets of the major players. They include billionaire tycoons, from oil moguls T. Boone Pickens (late) and Bill Anschutz, to the financial titan Warren Buffett.

While farmers and ranchers can earn a few thousand dollars for each turbine on their property, not everyone is so fond of these massive structures on the horizon. Darren Williams, one farmer I spoke with in Eastern Kansas, put it plainly. "I can't stand them." He said that when the wind developers came to town, they kept trying to convince him to put turbines on his farm. "It bothers me more that all the power is going to Kansas City. They came down to small-town America and put them out here because the people in the city don't want to look at them."

It's no surprise that when people don't have much of a say in the matter, they tend to not want a 300-foot piece of machinery looming over them, flickering the light as it spins. That is, unless they *do* have a say in the matter and the benefits are clear.

In South Dakota, Steve Sershen introduced a model of financing that put farmers first. It began two decades ago with a simple request for a car ride. "A group of farmers came to me 22 years ago. They were going to look at an ethanol plant and needed to borrow a Suburban." He'd just retired from a career in banking and thought he might as well give them a lift and check it out for himself. While the farmers were impressed with what they saw, the tour sparked a different idea. They already supplied the grain. Why couldn't they own the refinery?

From that notion, Steve set up a cooperative and raised $16 million from about 1,000 farmers and ranchers. Together they built the first farmer-owned ethanol plant in America. This bio-fuel refinery would go on to generate $250 million for the local economy. The experience took Steve from one project to the next, each focused on getting more value from agricultural products while using a producer-owned, co-op model. Over the next two decades, he'd go on to set up 51 companies this way. "They're all locally owned, small-business type stuff." In all, these ventures would invest $3.2 billion throughout the state.

When Basin Electric, the nearby electric co-op, wanted to set up a wind farm, Steve sought to give the farmers another opportunity. Over the course of dozens of townhall meetings throughout the state, South Dakota Wind Partners presented the project and invited locals to invest. In total, over 600 South Dakota residents raised $17 million in eight weeks. When it came time to make the case for the project to the Public Utility Commission, instead of protesting, people came out in support. Not everyone in town agreed with the proposal, but when they were given the opportunity to invest in something that affected their lives, they became natural advocates, rather than natural opponents.

This was not business as usual. Wind developers much prefer courting large banks and institutional investors. Most assume that having more investors is more work. But the experience of Nick Sershen, Steve's son who managed these relationships, didn't fit this assumption. "If we had one phone call a month, that was a pretty big month for the investors," he said. "The bigger players still don't understand that having a lot of smaller investors is just as easy as having one large investor."

Tax revenue from the turbines continues to make up 40 to 50 percent of the local township's budget, and they can now afford to plow the roads during snowstorms. "You're talking about local main streets that haven't created a new job in ten years, and now you're creating ten jobs in the area," said Steve. Crow Lake would go on to be the largest wind farm owned by a co-op, generating enough electricity to power nearly 60,000 homes.

Crow Lake's crowd-financed model is rare in the US, but in some countries, it *is* business as usual. In Denmark, 86 percent of the country's wind power is owned by co-ops, funded by over 100,000 families. In the Netherlands, the Zeewolde wind park plans to build nearly a gigawatt of generation with money from local farmers, neighbors, and a global network of small investors.

Solar financing is even easier to democratize, as projects reach economies of scale at one-hundredth the size of wind projects. SolarShare in Ontario sells bonds that pay a five-percent annual return to invest in solar projects throughout the province. Another company, Solstice, seeks to provide the benefits of solar to the 80 percent of Americans who can't put panels on their roofs. Known as "shared solar," with this model, several people invest in a larger project to offset their energy use. "It's kind of like a community garden, but for solar," said Solstice co-founder and CEO, Steph Speirs. Other energy co-ops concentrate the benefits with the community rather than individual investors or customers, using the profits to fund things like local infrastructure projects, climate change adaptation, or disaster relief funds.

On top of crowd-sourced financing models, there's a brand-new league of energy providers that seem to be doing all the things that traditional utilities have said were impossible. These innovative operators cut the cost of electricity, offer double the renewables, and pour surplus revenue back into the places they serve. These "community choice" programs allow groups of cities to band together and choose where their electricity comes from, what rates their customers pay, and how to spend their revenue.

In California, this new model was enabled by a voter-approved proposition on the state ballot. Marin Clean Energy (MCE) was the first community-choice provider to emerge. In less than ten years, they've doubled the renewables they offer compared to the utility, while reducing what their customers pay by five percent. Those savings would be closer to 30 percent if the utility didn't impose an exit fee on all monthly bills.

MCE is in the midst of a massive buildout of new wind and solar. It's an effort that will help them get to 100-percent clean energy by 2025, beating California's own ambitious statewide targets by 20 years. In the meantime, they give customers the choice to go 100-percent renewable immediately for a small premium. When I switched through my own local community choice program, it cost me around $3 more on my bill to essentially cut my carbon emissions by a third. And that premium often goes to build more renewable projects, some of which are focused on developing local jobs.

One project commissioned by MCE brought solar into the heart of old energy, and in doing so created new careers in the surrounding low-income community. Solar One was built on a reclaimed landfill, nested between the pipes and smokestacks of the Richmond Chevron Refinery. Nearly half of the workers who assembled the solar panels were city residents, many of whom had just graduated from a construction training program known as Richmond Build.

This program offers a free 12-week course where students learn construction, math, and receive a number of certifications. "We serve everyone: people in recovery, people who've been laid off, people with a history in the criminal justice system," said Fred Lucero, the organization's executive director. When students graduate, there's a direct pipeline into an apprenticeship in the trades and jobs on local public works projects.

For some in the area, this program is an alternative to organized crime. Richmond Build provides a way to develop skills and make a good living. "Nothing stops a bullet like a career," said Fred. "We totally believe that."

Jonathan Brito was one graduate of the program. He grew up in Richmond and, like other young people, had been in and out of the juvenile justice system from an early age. "My dad passed away when I was nine, so the streets were my dad," he said. For a decade, he painted cars for a living, but was concerned about the fumes he was breathing.

One day, he heard about MCE's solar project coming to his back-yard. "I wanted to do solar because I wanted to make the world a better place. For a year and a half, I called everyone, asking how I could get in-volved in the project." After completing the course at Richmond Build, he was one of the first to be hired onto the job that paid the prevailing wage of $50 an hour. The developer, Russel Pacific, then hired him and eight others full-time.

Solar One is one drop in a wave of new community choice programs sweeping the California grid. Today, over half of the state's residents get their power from one of 23 such organizations.

Each program is meant to meet the unique needs of each area. The Clean Power Alliance in Los Angeles promotes electric transportation to reduce the haze in the smog-plagued San Fernando Valley. Silicon Valley Clean Energy tailors their offerings to the majority of electricity that flows to commercial office parks. Pioneer Community Energy, located in the fire-prone foothills of the Sierra Nevada, not far from where the town of Paradise burned to the ground, is exploring ways to harvest the region's highly flammable dead trees for fuel in power plants that use wood waste to generate electricity. They want to convert a local hazard into a resource and a tool to reduce the risk of forest fires.

Regardless of whether you support or oppose the priorities of your community choice provider, you can walk right into an executive board meeting and speak your mind. I visited two such meetings as an ordinary citizen. It's something I couldn't imagine doing before the board of any privately owned utility company. Of course, not everyone will know the nitty-gritty of local energy policy, but there are independent organizations dedicated to ensuring that community choice keeps its focus on community. The East Bay Clean Power Alliance is one of those groups. I watched them advocate for my community-choice agency to double the amount of their annual surplus that they spend on local development projects.

It was here that I met Jessica Tovar, who leads their organizing efforts. Her journey into environmental justice began with her experience as a child in Los Angeles. "I grew up in housing projects that were near hundreds of polluting facilities: power plants, rendering plants, crematoriums, and a huge slaughterhouse," she recalled.

"Growing up, I had a lot of headaches and allergies and issues with concentrating. My mom developed breast cancer; she survived. My grandma developed breast cancer; she died. It was kind of a thing in my neighborhood where people were feeling the effects of living in an environment like that." She worked as an organizer for 16 years, challenging polluters who push the ill-effects of the economy onto low-income communities.

Today, she works to ensure a bright energy future for all. "We want to build local clean power infrastructure, create jobs, stimulate the economy, and keep that money circulating." Months later, when I checked in on her progress, she and a team of mostly volunteers had succeeded in securing $5 million for community projects—five times what the community choice agency had originally proposed.

The question is no longer whether we can harness wind and sun to turn the gears of our modern economy, but how that power enriches the communities it electrifies. The ever-present abundance of this energy allows more people to more easily capture and direct the wealth it creates over a wider landscape. From prairie to metropolis, the revolution behind the meter can begin building new and distributed wealth for generations to come.

---

**KEEP EXPLORING**

- *Where does my power come from and who benefits from its revenue?*

- *What organizations near me are advocating for local clean energy?*

- *What would it look like if the electricity that powered my home grew wealth for my community?*

---

# THE FUTURE IS ELECTRIC

THE GRID THAT POWERS OUR BUILDINGS IS ONLY HALF OF THE ENERGY equation. The other half can be found in the gasoline that moves us. We've tied the entire movement of people and goods everywhere on Earth to just one commodity. Changes in the price of oil don't just affect us at the pump, but at every cash register and online checkout page. It's in the cost of shipping, the cost of plastics in our products, and the cost of the fertilizer used to grow our food. Much of our modern economy runs on oil, which exposes us to a great deal of risk. Instability in one region half a world away can make the difference between debt and savings for millions of people. The only way to truly escape this cycle is to electrify our transportation. It's a big task, but one that may revolutionize access to mobility, while empowering a new workforce to make it happen.

Years before Ryan Popple made it his mission to free transit from its petro-dependence, he commanded tanks in the US Army. He was commissioned as an armored cavalry officer in 2000. It was "the last year of *Pax Americana.* The Cold War was over, the Berlin Wall had come down, there wasn't really a whole lot of bad stuff happening in the world," he recalled in an interview with Emily Kirsch of Power House. "But the fit hit the shan on 9/11." Everything changed, and "we knew things were getting real for us when desert-colored gear started getting dropped off."

One of their next deployments was Kuwait. They then pushed into Iraq in 2003. "The infantry division I served with landed in Normandy in 1944. I look at some of those photos and think, *we didn't have it that bad.* At the same time, there are friends of mine who are not here anymore."

When he returned, Ryan was able to find his way to business school, then to Tesla as one of the first 200 employees, and eventually Proterra, which is the largest electric bus company in North America. While he's faced challenges in his civilian career, his experience in war has put things into perspective. "You're not going to run into anything in the business world that's like a bad day over there."

As the CEO of Proterra, he sees beyond building a better bus. His larger goal is to revolutionize public transit by saving it from a financial death spiral. When the cost of running busses becomes too expensive for a transit agency, it's often forced to cut down on service, which causes more people to trust transit less, and eventually avoid it altogether. According to Ryan, using electricity over diesel to power a bus can reduce the cost per mile by 50 to 80 percent. His goal is not just to make transit environmentally sustainable, but economically viable.

Fuel-cost reductions and price stability can have huge benefits for transit agencies. By dramatically lowering the cost per mile, they can increase bus frequency or open routes that wouldn't have previously been economical. The electric motor also makes for a much quieter bus, about the same volume as an average conversation. This quiet ride, combined with the elimination of diesel fumes, may also make it easier to permit new lines.

The implications for riders are deeper. With less money needed to run busses, electric drive makes free public transit more viable. "If you lower the cost of transit, you can get rid of fareboxes. You can get rid of payment-card systems, and basically wherever you are in a city, every five to ten minutes an electric bus should come along." Ryan pointed to

Park City, Utah, and Missoula, Montana—places that have made public transit free and built the costs into other taxes. "We don't charge people a cost per mile to use the sidewalk. We have the infrastructure and we have a way of taxing a community for that service."

Beyond price savings, swapping diesel for electric power can provide serious benefits to public health. Higher rates of asthma and respiratory illness are often found along bus routes and trucking corridors. According to a Duke University study, if the cost of hospitalization and early death from diesel emissions were paid for at the pump, it would raise fuel prices to nearly $8 per gallon. Eliminating these fumes could alleviate the suffering of millions, as well as the cost to the healthcare system.

Proterra's busses, some of which can go over 1,000 miles on a single charge, are now in over 40 cities across the US. The company has also worked with Seneca, South Carolina, to make their entire fleet electric. Improvements in the technology and cost of new batteries have enabled more and more cities to set ambitious goals of moving to 100-percent electric transit.

Ryan sees the electric bus as the first crack in oil's ironclad dominance. "We are in the first market where fossil fuels are going to lose 100 percent of their market share. I don't think there are many companies who look at that 800-pound gorilla of fossil fuels and say, 'I'm going to take this entire market away from you, and there's nothing you can do about it.'"

To put the current energy transition into perspective, he compared it to the demise of the whaling industry in the 19th century, which was put out of business by kerosene lanterns. "If the whaling industry today had as much influence as the fossil fuel industry does today, we'd be trying to come up with synthetic whales so that we could support Nantucket and New Bedford," he said. "At one point, it no longer made sense to throw harpoons at aquatic mammals for energy." The same may become true of drilling pockmarks into the Earth to harvest liquified dinosaur bones.

Electric busses are only the beginning. "I think of what we're doing like island-hopping. And the smallest island, the easiest one to take over is the transit bus market. You use that as a launching point to show that you can take on bigger, heavy-duty markets." In the US, there are only about 65,000 public-transit busses on the road. Compared to cars, converting our bus fleets to electric appears more doable. And Ryan pointed out that "a lot of the policy that's looking to electrify trucks is looking at the positive experience of cities using electric transit busses as a proof point." Broad success in public transit could then inspire the electrification of the two million semitrucks, 450,000 school busses, and 136,000 garbage trucks that lumber down our streets.

But what of the 300 million personal cars in which most Americans get around? For the past three years, I'd been telling Greg that I would switch to an electric car like he did. They accelerate like a rocket ship, cost almost nothing to maintain, and don't even have a tailpipe. There are now several models close to my price range that can go over 200 miles on a single charge. But for all the benefits of owning an electric car, it was difficult for me to actually use one. Without a garage, there was no convenient place for me to charge. This single issue might be the most common mental hurdle to buying an electric car. Across the entire country, there are just over 17,000 public chargers—one-tenth the number of gas stations. If we're going to make electric cars viable, then the public charger will have to become as common as the parking meter.

While installing 100,000 high-voltage power connections may seem daunting, it also presents us with an opportunity. A new workforce may rise, empowered with the skills to build this electric infrastructure, as they free our transportation sector from sole dependence on one costly commodity. Already, the US solar industry employs more people than oil and coal extraction combined. It's a change that happened in less than a decade.

Alvaro Sanchez stands at the crossroads of gas and electric. He's worked for years transforming the seemingly mundane world of infrastructure into a creator of new careers. As a child, his family migrated back and forth between Los Angeles and Mexico City, attempting to stay afloat financially. Those struggles planted a question in his mind and a direction in his life. "How do we create prosperity for those excluded from economic opportunity?"

When he worked as a city planner, Alvaro saw every dollar spent on building our world as an opportunity to empower the people who live in it. Working at Green for All, he led a campaign to convince water utilities to invest in stormwater control, while also investing in people. "If it's ratepayer money, if it's taxpayer money, then you can put a lot of stipulations into what other things that money should do."

He worked to direct some of the funds spent on water infrastructure into hiring people in low-income communities. "Some folks might gain access to jobs through planting trees or cutting concrete. Eventually, there would be a pipeline to get into water utility jobs by learning more skills, as an apprentice." Many people working for utilities are baby boomers preparing to retire. Alvaro wanted to make equity a priority in hiring the next generation of utility workers. "From water pipelines to pipelines out of poverty," Alvaro laughed, "it's really hard not to use water puns."

Now at the Greenlining Institute, one of his newest projects is to take the same thinking and apply it to electric vehicle-charging infrastructure. He helped craft a piece of legislation to ensure that some of the money California spends on incentivizing sales of electric vehicles goes to programs that cater to people earning lower incomes.

For years, the primary beneficiaries of electric vehicle subsidies were those who could afford to buy a Tesla. But in reality, most air-quality issues caused by transportation affect low-income communities. To make up for the mismatch in funding and need, Alvaro said, "There are now several programs that allow low-income folks to scrap their polluting vehicles and get incentives to purchase new or used electric vehicles."

But Alvaro pointed out that we can't have electric vehicles in low-income communities if we don't have the charging infrastructure. When the California Public Utilities Commission approved $700 million in charging infrastructure, the Greenlining Institute negotiated with the state's three utilities to invest a certain amount of that money in economically disadvantaged neighborhoods.

Alvaro argued that it's not enough just to invest in new infrastructure. It's important to go deeper, and look at how that investment is spent and what it does in the communities it touches. We need to "incentivize the hiring of folks from those local neighborhoods to be able to work on the actual infrastructure. Or for small businesses to be able to gain access to contracts in the deployment of that infrastructure." It's reminiscent of Richmond Build's work in providing a pathway into construction, solar, and the middle class.

"Just changing the energy source from fossil fuels to renewable energy doesn't eliminate oppression," said Alvaro. "None of that happens if there aren't people involved in ensuring that the clean-energy economy is a more *just* economy." Greenlining continues to work with utilities to make this dream a reality. Their vision is to tie the rise of electric mobility to economic opportunity.

This new workforce may lay the foundation that liberates the economy from dependence on oil. The world that emerges may save us money at the pump while keeping millions out of the hospital through the elimination of harmful emissions. And as we hop off a free ride, we may notice something deeper. The noises and smells of our cities may begin to change, as rattling motors and diesel fumes are replaced with a clean electric hum.

## KEEP EXPLORING

- *Who's working to make emission-free transit a reality in my community?*

- *How might the electrification of transportation create new jobs in my community?*

- *Does the infrastructure exist for me to use an electric car? If not, who's building it?*

# GARDENS IN THE COALFIELDS

F OR GENERATIONS, HUNDREDS OF THOUSANDS OF WEST VIRGINIA COAL miners earned a good living. The money they made supported local economies in towns across Appalachia. And their labor down in deep mines brought light to the rest of the world.

But this prosperity came at a high price. Mountains were blown to pieces, rivers ran orange with mine tailings, and generations of miners suffered from black-lung disease. For over a century, the coal industry dominated the region's economy and psyche, preventing much else from taking root. Now, it's crumbling. Three of the four largest coal companies that mine half the coal in the US have gone bankrupt. There's a gaping hole in parts of Appalachia where an economy used to be.

The transition away from extractive energy, dependent on a few commodities, is not as simple as retraining miners. "You can have training programs until you're purple, but if you don't have a place to work, it's just kind of mean," said Marilyn Wrenn, the development director at Coalfield Development. "It's not like you can move out of coal mining and go work for the big data firm that opened up down the street." Recovery from the legacy of coal's decline requires a thorough regeneration of local economies from the ground up.

On one abandoned surface mine, a new story has emerged. A tractor dragged a piece of machinery, scraping its way along the scattered remains of a former mountain. A crew member pushed the accelerator, and a stone crusher chewed through the rubble. "It's eating these rocks and turning it into garden soil—and it's awesome," said Eva Jones, who drove the tractor.

The machine was capable of crushing stones up to 16 inches in diameter, and in one day, could make up to three acres of soil. In the new dirt, another crew planted an orchard. It was a mix of blackberries, hazelnuts, lavender, and pawpaws. Sustainably managed chickens, hogs, goats, and honeybees grazed and pollinated the half-farm, half-forest. Over time, these practices will capture carbon in the soil and generate income for the local West Virginians who farm the former minelands.

These efforts were the work of two enterprises founded by Coalfield Development—an organization that seeks to restore economic diversity in a region long beholden to the wealth of just one commodity. "Whether you think coal is a good thing or a bad thing, it's not wise to have all your eggs in one basket," said Coalfield's founder, Brandon Dennison.

Before starting Coalfield, he used to lead service trips to repair dilapidated houses in his home state of West Virginia. He remembered the day that changed his perspective. During one project, two shirtless men approached him with tool belts slung over their shoulders. They asked for paid construction work. Brandon had to tell them there were no jobs. "They were really motivated, they wanted to learn, and they wanted to work ... but because of where they lived, they didn't have an opportunity to apply that gumption."

Brandon became inspired to create Coalfield Development to provide that opportunity. He started with a construction company. They rehabilitated rundown buildings into affordable housing and new businesses—this time hiring people who needed jobs. From there, Coalfield grew into separate social enterprises that include land reclamation, construction, organic farming, woodworking, tourism, and solar installation.

These diverse businesses collaborate as a team in their mission to regenerate the economy from every angle. Reclaim Appalachia terraformed an old surface mine to get it ready for Refresh Appalachia to grow food. Meanwhile, Reclaim collected stones and wood from the site, which Revitalize Appalachia reused in the construction of new housing on the former mineland. Rediscover Appalachia crafted furniture from reclaimed wood to furnish the new homes, while Rewire Appalachia installed solar panels on the roof.

Coalfield Development uses a non-profit model because the area lacks the basic infrastructure needed for the private sector to create jobs. Part of their funding comes from public grants from the state of West Virginia and private contributions. The other part comes from the revenue generated by their businesses. As Marilyn said, "We're making revenue that we're reinvesting back into the economic infrastructure that under normal circumstances would have existed if one extractive industry hadn't put its giant foot on top of everything."

As Coalfield kickstarts the infrastructure for a new economy, they seek to revitalize the people building it. Of the more than 50 crew members across their enterprises, all follow a weekly schedule, known as the 33-6-3 model. It's 33 hours of paid work, six hours of tuition-free college classes, and three hours of personal development and counseling. As crew members build skills through their jobs, they work toward a two-year associate's degree at a local community college or technical school. They also get access to much needed services, like zero-interest loans deducted from their paychecks. "If something happens and medications go up one month and they have to choose between having medications or having electricity, we can help," said Marilyn.

The true wealth of Appalachia isn't underground, but within its people. Coalfield elevates the Appalachian values of "gumption, grit, and grace." They're the same qualities that allowed people to make a living in the mountains for generations. "This is us. We're figuring it out. It's not a solution that's been thrust upon us. We're making it work and we're making it in a way that fits within our communities and culture," Marilyn said. "We really do in Appalachia hold the key to a lot of these traditional skills that people are going to need … We grow things, we build things, and we fix things really well."

Coalfield provides employment and personal development while also creating a pathway to opportunities outside of their enterprises. One crew member was able to use the money she made working for Refresh Appalachia to leave an abusive relationship. She went on to get her associates degree and find a job working in agriculture in another part of the state. A young man who learned carpentry with Revitalize Appalachia was hired for a high-paying union construction job.

The organization also works to create a pathway for those recovering from addiction. West Virginia has been hit particularly hard by the opioid epidemic and currently has the highest overdose death rate in the US. Coalfield partners with drug treatment providers to hire people in recovery and acts as an advocate among other employers for hiring those who've struggled with addiction.

Even in dark times, the future of Coalfield looks bright. They recently purchased an abandoned factory, which they're refurbishing into their new headquarters. The Revitalize crew is fixing it up, while Reclaim has salvaged the yellow-pine flooring, selling it to local restaurants and bars. Refresh is working on an indoor mushroom and microgreen grow operation. Rediscover will relocate their woodshop. They also acquired SustainU, a clothing company that makes T-shirts for Major League baseball out of recycled cotton and plastic. They'll be relocating their printing and packing operations to the new space. On the roof, Coalfield is installing the largest solar array in West Virginia.

IN THIS SECTION OF THE BOOK, WE'VE SEEN A PATH FROM EXTRACTIVE towards renewable energy emerging. Changemakers are using the energy transition to raise the fortunes of many, balance the forces of wind and sun on a symbiotic grid, create a transportation system free from unstable commodities, and regenerate communities once dependent on fossil fuels.

But there's still something left unsaid. From every solution grows other potential challenges. The focus of the clean energy movement has been a crusade against the beast of "dirty fossil fuels." But what do we want the legacy of "clean energy" to be?

In terms of its ecological footprint, solar power is an immeasurable improvement over electricity generated by burning fuel. Yet when we look at the life cycles of solar panels and batteries, they aren't without their flaws. At the end of their useful lives, solar panels will sit in landfills or be shipped overseas to be stored in somebody else's backyard. Toxic chemicals like cadmium and gallium, along with battery acid from energy storage, present environmental problems of their own, not to mention all the mining required to produce these exotic materials.

We begin to see the true nature of the beast. The problem is not just fossil fuels themselves, it's how our economy and industries fundamentally operate. We dig, deplete, and discard. That's how we've done things for as long as we can remember. It's easy to forget, though, that this human system is an exception to nature's rule. All around us, and since the first bacteria burst into being, the world has always been based on the endless regeneration of *abundant* natural resources. That's exactly what we seek to rediscover in the next section of this book.

## KEEP EXPLORING

- *How can we regenerate the economy left behind by the fall of fossil fuels?*

- *What are the industries in decline in my community and how does it affect local people?*

- *What are the values in my community that might help cultivate an enduring, prosperous future?*

PART TWO

# Industry

—

"It's not an investment
if it kills the planet."

—VANDAVA SHIVA

I NEEDED NEW RUNNING SHOES. FOR THE PAST FEW YEARS, I'D BEEN training with the track team at Laney College, where I teach, and competing at national meets. Running is important to me, but I'm also an environmentalist. I told Trevor that I was bothered by the thought of buying new training shoes and just tossing the old pair in a landfill.

Swirling in my mind was the vision of a trash monster in the ocean—the Great Pacific Garbage Patch. Each year the world makes 300 million tons of plastic, a portion of which ends up in our oceans. I thought about the materials in my worn-out shoes and didn't want to continue feeding the problem. I couldn't stop picturing those images of dead birds with stomachs full of random plastic pieces and bottle caps, or turtles and dolphins caught in discarded nylon nets.

So I'd been eyeing a new kind of shoe to soothe my conscience. To my delight, I found a shoe that's forged out of plastic reclaimed from the ocean. Such a simple idea: repurpose harmful waste into elegant new products. My dilemma was solved.

But then I paused for a second to look at the bigger picture. We harvest raw materials from nature. We make something. We use it. We throw it away. We go through this linear sequence over and over but we never close the loop. Everything from food to consumer products to appliances and electronics is simply piled up in giant landfills as if it's worthless.

If we look closer, however, we realize that we don't actually have a *waste* problem at all. Waste doesn't exist in nature. It's an entirely human-made concept. Nature recycles everything, as the leftovers from one process become the building blocks for another. When one organism dies, it becomes fertilizer for the next generation of life. Ashes to ashes, dust to dust. It's a constant rhythm of growth, death, fertilization, and rebirth. It's the circle of life.

Rather than a waste problem, what we have is a *value* problem. We don't recognize the evergreen value within the products that we throw away. We often forget that "waste" contains the raw materials for new products, and that has enormous value. It's not the trash itself, but how we think about it that's the issue. Each year in the US alone, we throw away enough wood to heat 100 million homes for a decade, enough aluminum to re-build all commercial airliners four times over, and enough plastic bottles to wrap around the Earth 100 times over. Even used clothing—14 million tons of which ends up in the trash—could be remade into new clothes.

We can complete the circle. The front end of the economy can be connected to the back end in a continuous loop. We can think of our production cycles like the nutrient cycles that exist in nature. Jenine Bey-nus, the author of *Biomimicry*, advised looking to nature as a mentor in developing human technology. Using the "circle of life" as a mentor, we can create the "circle of stuff."

The idea of a circular economy is not new and has existed for tens of thousands of years. Centuries ago in parts of the Amazon, some societies composted their food, sewage, charcoal, and waste so effectively that they converted massive swaths of depleted tropical soils into nutrient-rich "terra preta" or "black earth," which is still observable to this day. These fortified soils allowed them to feed settlements of up to 100,000 people. In Europe during the Middle Ages, certain forests were tended like gardens to ensure consistent wood for fencing and housing. All around the world, people have altered environments to provide for their economies, but have often done so with the principles of regeneration.

Today, our materials and populations are far beyond anything our ancestors could have imagined. But so is our technology. It's time to innovate in alignment with timeless values. If we seek to ensure continuous, plentiful resources that don't pollute the Earth beyond recognition, we'd be wise to approach modern industry with a circular mindset. Of course, we may alter ecosystems in the process, but we can do so while thinking of the next millennia, rather than just the next fiscal quarter. In the following chapters, we hear from innovators who are reimagining our economic systems with regeneration as their guide.

# INDUSTRY AS AN ECOSYSTEM

———

WHEN WE FIXATE SOLELY ON CUTTING OUT WASTE, THE OUTLOOK for the environment can be discouraging. It seems we'll need a million campaigns to save our planet from discarded items as simple as plastic straws to those as complex as lithium-ion batteries. If we look closer though, we find that ecosystems themselves hold the key to their own preservation. When we learn from the way nutrients are constantly broken down and repurposed in natural systems, we find opportunity everywhere.

Bubbling in natural geysers all over the world—such as the hot mud of Old Faithful—there's a creature that's made a home for itself. It's a bacteria called *Methylocystis parvus*, and it feeds on the methane released from plants decaying in slow motion. For over 200 million years, these organisms have evolved in a microscopic ecosystem where the main energy source is a gas.

Dr. Allison Pieja spent years in the labs at Stanford studying how these bacteria work. She published extensively on how they use methane to build long chains of complex polymers. It was during her PhD studies that she met Dr. Molly Morris, who was working on sustainable materials for the construction industry. "It turns out that Molly's work needed Allison's work, and Allison's work needed Molly's work," said Dr. Anne Schauer-Gimenez, who would later join their team.

When you picture startups in the San Francisco Bay Area, you might think of a hip coworking space with cold-brew coffee on tap and walls plastered with inspirational quotes by Steve Jobs. The office of Mango Materials is a little different. I let Greg know that I'd be happy to check it out for both of us.

The road reached a dead-end at the Redwood City wastewater treatment plant and the smell was as you might expect. Anne welcomed me through the gates. We put on hard hats and walked down a set of stairs, following a network of metal pipes to an outdoor expanse of giant concrete drums. They were biodigesters that used bacteria to break down waste into a form that doesn't make us sick. Another set of pipes connected one of the digesters to a much smaller ten-foot-tall cylindrical chamber. This, I was told, is where the magic happens.

Methane from the digester enters the chamber where it feeds a colony of hungry bacteria. At first, they start dividing like crazy. Their numbers surge as they colonize this new habitat. Then, with a few twists of the knobs, they're cut off from their food source. They go into survival mode, building up an energy reserve for later. This energy reserve is made from the exact compound of an extremely versatile biopolymer, an ideal building block for a wide range of plastics. The Mango team then harvests the crop of microbes, leaving a seed group behind for the next batch. From the microbes, they extract a fine white powder, which they pelletize and then inject into plastic molds.

All the waste from the process is fed back into the biodigester. It's broken down with everything else, releasing the methane within, which is then looped back into the beginning of the cycle.

The plastic that comes out is different from plastic as we know it. Because it's a naturally occurring substance, it's easily broken down. Where most compostable plastic on the market has to be processed in industrial-scale composting facilities, these polymers can biodegrade in the yard. "We've done some very unscientific studies in our CEO's home compost," said Anne. More importantly, this polymer can decompose in the ocean. If an animal happens to eat it, they're able to digest it.

There are also many more applications for these polymers than for most of the existing biodegradable plastic on the market. The bacteria can produce over 100 different monomers—the building blocks of plastic polymers—allowing for plastics of many forms. "It's inherently a more rigid plastic. It's great for electronic casings or things that need to be durable," said Anne. "But you can also make it into thin, flexible films. It has a huge design space. You just have to know how to do it." That's what Mango has spent the last eight years figuring out.

The current plastics industry has a huge advantage as all the infrastructure is already set up, which allows existing companies to produce at a very low price. However, Anne pointed out that there are 1,200 facilities in the US that generate natural methane and already have some system to capture it. To avoid releasing it into the atmosphere, most places just burn it. At best, they can get a few cents per kilowatt hour for the power produced, if they happen to have a generator on site. Using methane to make plastic would create significantly more value.

According to Anne, "We're three times more economical than electricity and two times more valuable than converting that methane into liquid fuel."

Mango provides a dual solution. They prevent heat-trapping methane from escaping into the atmosphere as a greenhouse gas, while significantly reducing the harm done by plastic in our environment. At the same time, they present a powerful incentive for methane emitters to transform a harmful waste stream into a source of revenue.

This technology creates a new way to look at recycling altogether. Even if your bio-plastic bottle were to end up in the landfill—if that landfill were connected to one of Mango's systems—it would decompose back into methane. There, it could be captured and transformed back into another plastic bottle. It's essentially a biological recycling system that could help us reconceive landfills as not the end of the line for our products, but the beginning. Sites not for waste, but for value creation.

Mango envisions a new approach to infrastructure that is significantly less capital-intensive. Rather than establish massive plastic factories, Mango wants to license mobile modules that can plug into any source of methane and start producing immediately. Imagine if every city had its own source of extremely versatile materials made from the sweet nectar of benevolent bacteria. It's a rose-colored dream compared to relying on the concentrated byproducts of petrochemicals that are shipped across plastic-choked seas.

Mango uses biology to re-envision the way we make things. It's what's called a "biocycle." But not all industrial systems that copy the way nature regenerates materials have to use biology. There's another cycle that uses artificial means to do what natural nutrient cycles do so well. It's been dubbed the "technocycle" by architect William McDonough and chemist Michael Braungart, the authors of *Cradle-to-Cradle*, who helped popularize a vision for circular industry. The "technocycle" includes basically all manufactured products that can't be broken down by nature. These materials are persistent and often toxic, like heavy metals. When they do end up in nature, they're what we call pollution.

It's possible, though, to find ways of safely breaking them down. Rather than letting them destroy our environment, we can keep them in circulation, where they create value rather than destruction. For a glimpse of what that might look like, we now turn to the fastest-growing waste stream on the planet.

While shiny and sleek on the front end, our tech industry has created a monster on the back end. Each new gadget kicks millions of older models into obsolescence. Discarded electronics get shipped by the crateload to the developing world, where their toxic components can poison entire neighborhoods. In Bangladesh, children dip circuit boards into open vats of acid to get at the copper and gold nested inside. In the Congo, warlords use slave labor to mine the cobalt that supplies the world's battery manufacturing.

Before Peter Holgate learned of the dark side of Moore's Law, he'd founded several companies in the tech space. However, it wasn't until he received a letter from his mother that he'd come to chart a different path. "The last thing in the letter was that she'd met Michael Musk, Elon Musk's uncle, and Michael told her that Elon had built a rocket ship which flew into space and landed square on a platform in the Pacific Ocean. And then she goes, 'How's your career coming along?'"

But before Peter had a chance to respond, she passed away. In the months of grief that followed, he couldn't stop thinking about what his mother would've wanted his impact on the world to be.

During this time, he happened to watch the documentary *Ghana: Digital Dumping Ground*. In it, he saw how his career in tech might be contributing to a looming problem. He became inspired, not to create the newest gadget, but to figure out what to do with those gadgets when they're disrupted by the next big thing. "You've got phenomenally good-looking devices, and these things do well, they're powerful. You've got stores that are amazing. They're like a temple, right? And yet, you haven't been giving the back end enough attention."

So Peter went searching for solutions. Rather than try to invent a new technology from scratch, he suspected that the tools to address the problem might already be out there. He stumbled across a strange piece of equipment built for an entirely different purpose. At the time, it was languishing in the tent of an environmental remediation company. It was a machine made up of a 13-foot-long steel bar surrounded by electromagnets. It's "basically a massive tuning fork," originally built to "literally shake the gold out of mine tailings using sound energy."

This sonic machine is extraordinarily efficient at separating materials, especially when compared to smelting—the main method for recovering metals from our discarded electronics. Traditional recycling uses an arc plasma furnace to melt everything down, which requires a tremendous amount of power, often generated by burning coal. By contrast, the tuning fork technology separates the mélange of materials in a circuit board by using what's known as "harmonic resonance."

"When you go 'ping,' the tuning fork is humming and you just add a touch of energy, just to keep it at that rhythm and state, a harmonic state." From this technology, Peter and his partners founded Ronin8, a company focused on creating a circular life for electronic devices.

At their facility, old laptops, monitors, and cell phones enter the process whole. They're shredded under water to prevent toxic dust from escaping into the air. These minced bits of e-waste are then fed into the machine, which fine-tunes its pitch to separate each material based on its specific density. First the non-metals are released. Finally, one by one, each metal resonates with its perfect harmony.

"We've found up to 21 different metals in most electronics. It's like the entire periodic table. Even the guys who are recovering the primary metals—you know, gold, copper, silver, platinum, palladium—are ignoring most of the rarest elements, like promethium and tungsten," said Peter. "We started down the path of being able to recover all of them." Currently, mining these rare-earth metals requires an intensive chemical process to liberate them from the dirt. Often they're bound up with radioactive by-products like thorium, all of which end up seeping into the groundwater.

The current smelting process to recycle metals isn't able to recover these rare earth elements. In addition, it requires high levels of energy and emits toxic particles. "You create dioxins, which are the same thing you find in DDT and Agent Orange." The two main ingredients in Ronin8's process are sound and water. After the discarded electronic components have been separated, the remaining particles are filtered through a fine sieve and the water is reused indefinitely.

Peter hinted that the process might be well suited for recycling solar panels. "The entire solar panel industry is staring down at a legacy issue without the means to solve it," he said. "The solar panels that were built 15 to 20 years ago are all aged out and need to be taken down. These work incredibly well in our sonic system."

Currently, Ronin8's main focus is perfecting their technology to safely and affordably recycle lithium batteries. This could help address the looming specter of the millions of used electric car batteries that the world will come to generate every year.

Ronin8's goal is to develop partnerships with the big manufacturers. "We want to be their facilitator of the circular economy," said Peter. He sees the need for larger companies to fundamentally rethink their business models. "I see the brands as custodians of the circular economy, not as the sellers of gadgets." They're going to look at all the metal they have in their products, and say, "Look, we've deployed a hundred million tons of gold—or whatever the number is—and we are the steward to make sure it's going 'round and 'round."

Ronin8 also wants to provide an opportunity for people in the developing world who live where this waste falls through the cracks. They envision their technology being able to fit into a shipping container. "Instead of having some kid melt away the plastic to get at the copper, you have a simple, easy way to separate the two." It could give people living anywhere in the world the means to safely transform complex waste into a cornucopia of useful materials.

In nature, leaves and branches fall into streams and end up far away from their places of origin. But they don't pollute their new environments. Natural systems are adept at converting leaf litter into food, fertility, and new life. In our modern economy, we're not talking about branches and leaves, but circuit boards and copper wires. The material may be different, but our approach and intention when dealing with them should model nature's. Our goal should be to allow anyone, wherever they are, the opportunity to create value from the problem formerly known as pollution.

In the US, regenerating the value from discarded products could help bring back manufacturing jobs. James Killkelly, the founder of Apto Solutions, a company that dismantles electronics and repurposes their internal parts, sees a major opportunity on the horizon. "The good news is that a lot of the 'Rust-Belt' locations that have been left behind could really benefit from a more circular economy. This kind of work we're doing has the potential to revive American manufacturing."

Interestingly enough, this work can't be outsourced to China because the government there has banned the import of used goods. The backside of our economy may be a sleeping giant of job creation.

We've spent the last 100 years perfecting the assembly line. It's now time to perfect the *disassembly* line. Nature is able to take extremely complex structures and break them down into the pieces needed for the next generation. For everything we create, we need an efficient solution to break it down and cycle it back into the pieces from which it came. In doing so, we can create value out of nothing, protect the environment from toxic chemicals, and avoid depleting our precious natural resources.

---

## KEEP EXPLORING

- *What are the broken circles of stuff that I notice in everyday life?*

- *What treasure do I see ending up in the trash?*

- *How could my local economy endlessly regenerate all the materials it uses?*

# INFINITE WARDROBE

THIRTY YEARS AGO, THE ARAL SEA WAS THE FOURTH LARGEST LAKE IN the world, right behind Lake Superior. In the local Turkic languages of Uzbekistan and Kazakhstan, its name means "Sea of Islands." At one time, 1,100 islands rose above its waters, providing harbors for birds and boats. Today, those islands look similar to the mesas of Death Valley. Camels now find shade beneath the rusted hulls of old fishing vessels. The inland sea was drained to flood fields of cotton. Every year, it shrank more and more, until today, there's almost nothing left.

Behind this disappearance is a growing apparel industry propelled by "fast fashion." The fiber needed to constantly refresh our wardrobes outpaces the ability of natural systems to replenish themselves. The fashion industry produces about a tenth of the world's carbon emissions and is one of the largest industrial consumers of water. About 80 percent of garments are destined for the landfill, some of that ending up as microplastics in the ocean.

There are two ways to prevent this industry from consuming everything in its path. One way is to give the fiber in fast fashion multiple lives. The other is to slow down altogether and return this global system to its local roots.

It was a few decades into Stacy Flynn's career in textiles that she started to look more closely at the industry's impact. In doing so, she found two glaring problems. "The first was the resources for fiber are massive. Ninety percent of all clothing in the world is made from either cotton grown on land, or polyester pulled from the Earth's crust.

"Both types of fiber generation require massive resources. Seven hundred gallons of water are used to make a single cotton T-shirt. The $CO_2$ required to make polyester is enormous as well." The second thing was that on the back end, consumers in the US throw away 14 million tons of garment waste every year. "I saw the two bookends and the design challenge really became clear. Is there a way for us to take this waste and break it down and convert it into a high-quality fiber?"

As she went to work devising a system that might be able to make this happen, she very quickly ran into a major challenge. A batch of garment waste is a mix of many different fibers with residue from all the grime and detergent left over from a lifetime of use. However, the apparel industry is designed to work with one consistent stream of high-quality fiber. Stacy referred to this as the "cardinal rule" of the textile industry. The alternative system she envisioned would break it. When she first pitched her idea to potential partners and investors, all of them turned her down. "I can't tell you how many times I've had doors slammed in my face when I said I wanted to break that rule."

And then she pitched it to one of her former colleagues, Christo Stanev. "Christo was the only one who didn't slam the door in my face." They spoke for hours, and after going back and forth on all the challenges, he finally gave her a smidgen of hope.

"I don't know that it's impossible," he said.

They went on to found Evrnu on that premise. Over several years, they developed an entirely new technology that gives old clothing a second life. As Stacy put it, the process they created "liquifies cotton garment waste, and then extrudes it into a new fiber." She knew they were onto something when she "took a T-shirt from a solid to a liquid and then back into a solid with a syringe."

Remaking fiber in this way uses 98 percent less water compared to growing virgin cotton. For polyester, it cuts carbon emissions by 80 percent. In total, Evrnu's technology can get three additional lives from cotton fiber before it starts to break down into cellulose. At that point, it can be digested by the Earth.

As Evrnu perfects their recycling system, they're working with a number of top brands like Levi's and Stella McCartney. They're testing ways to make second-life fiber that has the exact qualities of virgin fibers. "If we can outperform virgin materials, or at least be on par, then, to a consumer, it would look no different and feel no different," she said. "That's the name of the game."

In the process, the fiber they've ended up creating has a number of interesting properties that could potentially make it more versatile. "Cotton naturally has one DNA molecule marker per grade of cotton. Our technology has multiple grades of cotton DNA, so we're not exactly sure what it will be called yet," she said.

"With it, we can simulate properties of cotton, silk, or rayon, and also some qualities of polyester." Evrnu is still fine-tuning their technology for recycling cotton, and has plans to tackle polyester next. Their end goal is not to produce their own fiber *en masse*, but to license their technology to textile manufacturers. That's why Stacy and Christo have designed their extruder to fit onto existing equipment.

While Evrnu's mission is challenging, Stacy feels like they're riding a wave of change. The machinery may still be the same, but the mindset within the industry is not. "In the past seven years working with this technology, I've seen a profound shift in consciousness. What I've seen is a fearlessness in the expression of love for humanity. It's so powerful. Because when people are unafraid to express their love for humanity, amazing things happen; the impossible becomes possible."

While Evrnu seeks to give the existing apparel industry a way to transform our old clothing into next season's line, Rebecca Burgess has taken a different path. She works to revive local textile economies that have been lost in the era of "fast fashion." Fibershed, the organization she founded, advocates for "slow fashion" and re-envisions the way we produce fibers, like a regional watershed or foodshed. While the global textile industry can degrade the land on a massive scale, Fibershed advances a system that heals our land at a local level.

She was inspired by the Indigenous basket weavers of Northern California and the wool-producing shepherds of her European ancestry. Both used fire to manage the health of grasslands across millenia. Studying with people from the Wintu, Ohlone, and Coast Miwok groups, she learned how "they were able to tighten the regenerative cycles" of specific grasses to make baskets and clothing. The abundance of material in their economy was directly tied to the health of the land.

When Rebecca opened her own wardrobe, she realized the connection between her clothing and the land was missing. Most of the fiber was produced in a way that degraded the soil and exploited the people who wove it. As a fiber artist, she felt a responsibility to use her skills to reconnect what she wore with the landscape. Her goal became to source all her clothing from within 150 miles of her home.

Pretty early on, she found something that shocked her. It wasn't the lack of local fibers, dyes, and talent. It was that the materials to make her new wardrobe were all around her. Every year in Northern California, one-and-a-half million pounds of wool are thrown away. There's a "glut of fiber." It's enough to supply everyone in the region with one wool item per year. But less than one percent is actually processed. Meanwhile, there's a lot of "talent pouring out of our design schools." The countryside produces more than enough fiber and the cities have the skillset. What's missing is the infrastructure to bring them together. That's what Rebecca set out to build.

She combined Merino wool from a 100-year-old rancher and the weaving skills of an 18-year-old fiber artist. Together they made a sweater, colored with natural dye from a local chaparral species. Rebecca also created a pair of jeans, bringing together an organic cotton farmer, an artisan weaver, and a designer from Levi Strauss. Rebecca pounded indigo leaves harvested from her own garden to produce blue for the denim. Within ten months, she'd brought together a once-isolated collection of local ranchers, weavers, and designers. This community became Fibershed.

Her next challenge was to expand beyond her own wardrobe—to make these products accessible to others. But to make anything at a commercial scale, fiber producers would have to ship raw wool to mills thousands of miles away. There were no mills in her state big enough to produce at any scale beyond handknitting. She explored what it would take to build a new mill, and the figure she arrived at was $28 million. She realized that she'd have to first prove the demand for locally grown clothing before she could convince prospective investors.

Fibershed assembled an unlikely team. They partnered with ranchers, soil scientists, and The North Face to create a new kind of wool—one that sequesters carbon in the ground by growing healthy soil in the pasture. Forty-some farms and ranches participated in the Climate Beneficial Wool program, which supplied high-quality fiber for a collection designed by The North Face. The clothing line featured a beanie, a scarf, and a jacket. The year it launched, that beanie was the company's top seller in its category. While these items were more expensive, they were designed to last for 30 years. A percentage of the proceeds funded practices that captured carbon in the soil and healed the land.

"We cannot rebuild local systems without using carbon as an organizing principle," said Rebecca. Carbon and water form the foundation of all natural fibers. The challenge is to produce those fibers in a way that supports the ability of plants to suck carbon out of the air and convert it into fertile ground and useful material. Fibershed identified 35 land-management practices for building soil carbon. A portion of the proceeds from Climate Beneficial Wool allowed the ranches to spread compost on the land as a slow-release stimulant of plant life, restore rivers and streams, graze sheep in a way that's friendly to the grass, and plant trees.

In the high desert of Surprise Valley, where California meets Nevada, Bare Ranch is using its beanie money to plant a mile-long windbreak. Made of native trees and shrubs, it will shield the sheep from sandstorms, provide a corridor for pollinators, and pump organic matter through their roots into the degraded soils. The Climate Beneficial Wool program spans operations of all sizes, from the second-largest ranch in California to a woman who herds sheep on just two acres.

Fibershed is working towards a future where "your clothes become a carbon sink." They estimated that if these farms and ranches continue to carry out carbon-farming plans over the next 20 years, they may sequester enough carbon to offset their operations by six to nine times what they emit. Rebecca pointed out that if the 45 participants were to increase soil carbon by just one percent on one percent of their land, "we could remove 333 million pounds of carbon from our atmosphere." It's the equivalent of offsetting 118,000 vehicles running for a year.

Looking beyond Northern California, Fibershed seeks to spread their model while staying true to their local philosophy. As the director of their affiliate program, Jess Daniels, put it, "We don't want to scale Climate Beneficial Wool and roll it out across the country and tell people what to do." Instead they work to incubate the local fibershed of each region. "We're providing a lot of transparency and open-sourcing the road map of what we've been doing, and then sharing that with communities." Today, there are nearly 50 affiliates across the world, from New York to Kentucky, and Ontario to Melbourne. Each is working to revive local fiber systems for wool, cotton, and hemp.

The main issue, of course, is affordability. The Climate Beneficial beanie goes for $60 and the wool jackets are $399. That's more than many people, Greg and I included, would be willing or able to spend. In breaking free from an industry based on cheap labor and materials, we can end up making inaccessible products. We substitute the exploitation of people and planet for a solution that only makes sense for a few people. How then do we reconcile this inherent contradiction?

One answer is rooted in personal values, rather than material ones. Do we value access to cheaply produced goods that last a few seasons, or high-quality goods that endure for decades? Fibershed's vision for "slow fashion" is about developing a deeper connection to the items we own. Rather than continuously buying the next thing, it's about acquiring cherished items that over the long run might end up saving us money. Meanwhile, the continued revival of local production that Fibershed nourishes may improve the economies of scale and hopefully make these items more affordable.

In seeking to clothe ourselves in a way that replenishes our resources and heals the land, we need solutions that enhance material and personal values. We need the tools to make the existing "fast-fashion" industry more circular, as the vast majority of clothing is made in this way. At the same time, we can revive a slower form of fashion—one that's focused on the quality, durability, and pride in what we own. Together these shifts may begin to restore degraded landscapes both in our own backyards and across the world.

## KEEP EXPLORING

- *What are my most prized everyday possessions and how do I take care of them?*

- *How do the things I buy impact the land?*

- *What would it look like if those impacts were positive?*

# IMMORTAL FOREST

WE TEND TO THINK ABOUT THE NEGATIVE IMPACT OF MANUFACTURing as waste from consumer goods and pollution from their production. But hiding in plain sight is something much bigger. In the relative blink of an eye, the construction industry can make a million trees disappear and turn mountains to dust. It transforms these timeless things into the places we call home. In the last century, over half of all resources consumed in the US and Europe have been used to build our cities and infrastructure. As the pace of global construction intensifies, it's important to bring this industry into harmony with the natural environment's ability to regenerate its resources. It may be possible for our built environment of wood and concrete to rise and fall like trees in a forest.

Concrete makes our world, while destroying another. "When you hear about mountain tops being blown off, that's usually not coal, that's rock," said Brent Constantz of Blue Planet, a company that's re-envisioning construction material. "After water, rock is the most moved material on Earth."

Every year, we mine 55 billion tons of the stuff, much of which is ground into aggregate that fuels construction. We dig up ancient reefs, whose sand provides a source of new material to create buildings that are only intended to last a few decades. When these structures come down, at best, the old concrete can be used as road base. At worst, the rubble is sent to landfills or dumped into the water. Currently, most old concrete isn't strong enough to be reused in new construction. We're forced to mine more rock every time.

Cement, the glue that holds the mass together, is no better. While it makes up just ten to 20 percent of what's in concrete, it alone is responsible for six percent of all human-made carbon emissions. That's because cement releases carbon at both ends of its making. We superheat limestone, often burning coal to do so. As the heat transforms the limestone into cement, it ejects carbon trapped within the rock itself.

Before Brent Constantz started thinking about concrete and cement, he got his PhD in marine biology, and he wrote his dissertation on coral formation. After his degree, he took his knowledge of how minerals form in nature and founded Norian. The company makes bone cement for orthopedic surgery in many operating rooms. Over the next few decades, he'd go on to hold over 100 patents for cement.

Rather than mining rock for concrete, Brent's newest company, Blue Planet, has found a way to grow it. In nature, limestone forms over millions of years from the skeletons of invertebrates, like coral and shellfish. Blue Planet can do the same in a matter of hours.

Their process begins in the smokestack of a natural-gas power plant. They start by diverting a stream of $CO_2$ and converting it into $CO_3$. Meanwhile, in another process, they harvest calcium from old concrete taken from demolition sites. That calcium acts like a seed and the $CO_3$ grows around it to become limestone. With that limestone, they now have the raw material for both cement and the aggregate rock to make concrete. The process they've invented prevents carbon from entering the atmosphere, keeps mountains from being mined, and diverts old concrete from being dumped into landfills.

Brent claimed that they can capture 80 percent of $CO_2$ emissions from a single source. While today, Blue Planet produces 70,000 tons of rock from one power plant, if applied at a global scale, their method could theoretically meet the demand for 55 billion tons of rock, while cutting nearly 80 percent of global emissions from factories and power plants.

The point, however, isn't to make this a silver-bullet solution for capturing emissions from every smokestack on the planet. What's important is to look at the places that will be very difficult to decarbonize. This space happens to be intimately tied to construction.

Steel and cement are extremely difficult to decarbonize. Not only do they require massive amounts of energy to produce, but the way they're made naturally releases carbon into the air. Together, they're responsible for 15 to 17 percent of global emissions. If we can turn this carbon into rock and mix it with calcium from old concrete, we can begin to reimagine a construction industry that resembles the life cycle of a forest. The rise and fall of buildings may come to copy the growth and death of trees. Demolition becomes like natural decomposition, as the rubble from old structures combines with carbon in the air to grow the next generation of homes and habitats.

This new approach would also allow us to access a large amount of building material locally. "Right now, the State of California projects we need about 12 billion tons of rock over the next 50 years. We only have about a third of the quarries available [in the state] to actually mine that rock. And so, even today, we're importing a lot of it from British Columbia. We have the ability to short-circuit that and reuse all of the rock in all of the concrete, so that we don't have to mine more of it." As Brent pointed out, "There's as much concrete demolished every year, or returned concrete, as there is new concrete laid down." Each city today may have most of the material it needs to rebuild itself countless times over.

Brent sees the power to create this future resting in the hands of the biggest users of concrete. "Government's strongest tool in curtailing $CO_2$ is not its power to tax $CO_2$. It's its power of procurement." A great deal of the concrete poured is in government-built roads, sidewalks, bridges, and airports. City, state, and federal agencies may have the power to choose concrete that costs the same, but comes from the air. In one of Blue Planet's first contracts, they're supplying the material for an expansion of San Francisco International Airport.

Brent emphasized that this solution has to work for everyone, everywhere. "It's financially sustainable and it's something you can do in a poorer country or a rich country. Any solution that doesn't work for the whole world doesn't count in my opinion. If it only works in Norway and Sweden and California, that isn't going to cut it." For a notoriously traditional and capital-intensive industry, any scalable solution will have to work seamlessly with the existing system. As Brent put it, "I don't want to have any equipment that's not already made by somebody else, that's not in inventory by five different vendors, because to scale you have to go out there and deploy rapidly."

Coming up with a groundbreaking new building material is relatively easy, compared to actually making it work within the risk-averse and highly regulated construction industry. Blue Planet's innovation is in adaptation with existing equipment. It may be one of the few ways to remix a destructive system into renewable cycles of cement, steel, and concrete—not unlike the water, carbon, and nitrogen cycles that sustain a forest.

But what about the forest itself? Wood is the oldest and most versatile building material. Trees don't need any tweaks to regenerate themselves in endless loops. They transform carbon in the air into homes in both the natural and human world, while simultaneously making much of the oxygen we breathe. Wood can be a renewable resource, as long as the way we harvest it doesn't outpace its regrowth.

Timber isn't always cut with regeneration in mind. About half of the global forest that existed 200 years ago has been cleared. Millenia ago, much of Europe was a forest, until it was used to build the Roman

Empire and countless nations and cities since then. Just three percent of the continent's old-growth forest remains. Logging can clearcut a million-year-old forest into a valley of stumps faster than a new seedling can set down its roots. While our machines can make quick work of timeless beauty, we're reminded of what Jeff Goldblum's character in *Jurassic Park* once said, "Life, uh, finds a way." Forests can come back. They've been practicing ever since the first fire turned them to ash and smoke. They can also be harvested responsibly in the wild or grown rapidly in tree farms.

But wood has its limitations. There are many things it can't do. It rots when exposed to water for long periods of time. It decays naturally and starts to lose its structural integrity. Redwood, cedar, and tropical hardwoods that *can* stand the test of time and hold up to the elements are expensive and often harvested from pristine, primary forests.

There is a way, however, to give common fast-growing wood uncommon strength. That's the mission of Pablo Van De Lugt, head of research at Accoya. "We've created wood without the weakness of wood," he said. Accoya has developed a non-toxic curing process that gives affordable pine the same qualities as tropical hardwood, or even aluminum siding.

When we see the words "tropical hardwood," our minds might go to illegal logging in the Amazon. But making raw aluminum can destroy forests as well. Bauxite, the ore mined for this metal, requires clearcutting and sifting through vast stretches of land. We then have to generate an immense amount of electricity to liberate aluminum hidden within the rock and soil. While aluminum is infinitely recyclable, currently the demand for second-life material outstrips the available supply.

Accoya wood can be used as a replacement for aluminum in construction. It's waterproof and guaranteed to last 50 years. It's rot-resistant and can be used to line canals. "We take something from the biocycle and make it as competitive as something from the technocycle," said Pablo.

Unlike aluminum or PVC, which will linger in the environment for thousands of years, Accoya wood will biodegrade at the end of its useful life. Before it gets to that point, it can be reborn as wood chips pressed into durable siding for another generation of housing. All the while, "during the time that wood has been in use, it's already grown back two times over." Because the sustainably harvested pines that Accoya uses grow so much faster than old-growth hardwood, they require ten times less land for the same amount of timber.

For centuries, the growth of the city came at the expense of the countryside. Today, we mourn the loss of mountains and primeval forest. But when the cycles of city growth come to resemble that of the forest itself, we may forge a more harmonious relationship between them. The wilderness that we preserve today will become the old-growth forests and ecosystems that our future descendants will wander through and marvel. By reimagining the way we build our cities, we can glimpse a more wild and prolific natural world in the future.

## KEEP EXPLORING

- *When I see a building torn down, what are the main materials being thrown away?*

- *What are some ways that wood, concrete, and steel can easily be reused locally?*

- *How might my city rebuild itself from the same stuff that made it?*

# PEOPLE, PLANET, PROSPERITY

—

IN THE SUMMER OF 2014, A YEAR BEFORE I MET TREVOR, I WAS RIDING through Costa Rica's remote Osa Peninsula. I was in search of one last local landowner to interview for my doctoral research project about managing forests. I'd gone as far as I could on horseback. I tied the horse and set out on foot into the steepest, least traversable stretch of mountainous jungle.

This section of Costa Rica is one of the world's biodiversity hotspots, with a large population of jaguars, 400 species of birds, 700 species of trees, and an amazing array of snakes and amphibians. It's so teeming with life that during a daily ride on my motorcycle, I would be plastered with butterflies and pelted with birds.

On this particular day, ascending the mountainside with my leather bookbag draped over my shoulder, my feet slipping on the wet red-clay soils while dodging some of the most venomous snakes on Earth, I thought, *Why did I come out here again?*

My mind wandered back to my geography PhD program at the University of Texas, Austin, where this adventure began. I'd been fed a healthy diet of theory about sustainable development, the human/environment relationship, and dogma from everyone from Adam Smith to Karl Marx. All social-science graduate programs obsessively philosophize about capitalism. One camp says that capitalism survives by sucking the life out of workers and nature, so we need to chuck the whole system. Those on the other side argue that completely unrestricted capitalist growth is the key to solving our biggest global problems.

At some point, theories weren't enough. What I truly craved was finding a real-world example where the economy, workers, and the environment all prospered within the same system. But was this win-win-win relationship even possible?

I ended up in Costa Rica to study something called "payment for ecosystem services," or PES. Rather than encouraging economic development by destroying nature—felling forests, damming rivers, and harvesting resources—PES programs do the opposite. Governments and private companies pay landowners of forested land *not* to cut down the trees on their property.

They do this because of a revolutionary concept: trees perform "ecosystem services" for humanity that have financially measurable benefits. How much does it cost to industrially filter a trillion gallons of water? Forests do it for free. How much would it cost to sequester billions of tons of $CO_2$ out of the air annually? Living trees do it in their sleep. The price to produce oxygen? The list goes on.

Right now, the value of ecosystems and the people who cultivate and harvest from them is too often exploited to provide profit for massive corporations. It's a trite subtext of modern capitalism. The Amazon is destroyed to feed cattle for distant consumers. Forests are cleared in Indonesia to grow palm oil for the global food industry. In West Africa, Cote d'Ivoire has lost over 80 percent of its rainforest in 50 years, most of which was cleared to grow cacao. Those who work the cacao farms typically get back just three to six percent of the price paid for a chocolate bar, and their families often end up living off $1 per person per day. Meanwhile, the manufacturers and retailers take home 80 percent of the revenue from an industry that does $100 billion in sales annually. Models like payment for ecosystem services along with fair trade seek to create a better relationship between workers, the market, and the environment.

I sat down with Mathieu Senard, co-founder of Alter Eco, a company that sources organic fair-trade cacao. "I've seen our fair-trade pricing allow farmers to rebuild critical roads, to build schools and water-wells, to pay for health care, and buy goats for the community," he said in the company's office in San Francisco's Mission Bay neighborhood. His company is showing that an environmentally and socially sustainable business model not only works, but can out-perform traditional business models.

Born in France, Mathieu is fluent in English, but still retains a mellifluous French accent. Before he entered the business world, he worked in refugee camps on the border of Cambodia and Thailand. His co-founder Edouard Rollet worked for UNICEF in Africa.

"Do you have kids?" he asked me as he adorned the table between us with dark chocolate bars, chocolate caramel balls, and coconut chocolate clusters.

"Yes," I replied.

"Kids love our stuff!" he assured me.

I asked Mathieu about the social impacts of Alter Eco. "Before fair trade," he said, "farmers were constantly at the mercy of wildly fluctuating international commodity prices. If the cost to produce a pound of coffee, for instance, is $1 just for argument's sake, the fair-trade price will always be a certain percentage above that cost, say $1.25. But the international price can easily be down to 50 cents for a few years, so these farmers go deep into debt if they are not guaranteed a livable price through fair trade. All the while, retailers continue to sell at the same price, so they make huge profits while the people at the bottom suffer."

Beyond guaranteeing more money to farmers through minimum pricing, Alter Eco has started projects to reforest a portion of the Peruvian Amazon. They do this not just by replanting trees, but by bringing the forest to the farm.

Rather than a monoculture of cacao trees, the Acopagro farming co-op that supplies their beans practices a form of cultivation known as dynamic agroforestry. They mimic the rainforest by planting four levels of growth with cacao trees on top, mango, yucca, and banana in the middle, nitrogen-fixing trees below, and plots of beans and corn shaded by the canopy above. The result increases local biodiversity, cacao production, food security, and resilience in the system. In the dry season, the banana stalks actually provide water for the cacao trees to grow without additional inputs. Farmer income has grown by 20 percent, and they refer to the new trees not as something to be cleared for short-term survival but as their "retirement plan." Every year, Alter Eco, the cacao co-op, and the PUR Project collaborate to plant 200,000 new trees in the Amazon.

Mathieu leaned forward and picked up a bag of sweets. "And another thing, soon all of our packaging will be biodegradable as well."

He spoke of both the challenges and the opportunities of looking beyond profit as the only indicator of success. "To be frank, we gross over $20 million a year, but we still have difficult financial decisions to make. On one end, we are like any other company, yet we self-impose rules that make us spend much more than mainstream companies for packaging, raw materials, labor, and even things like being 100-percent carbon neutral. The challenge is always striking a balance between doing the right thing and staying above water financially. It's the story of our 15 years. The bet, we think, is that this is what people are going to increasingly demand."

He's right. In recent years, companies like Danone, Walmart, Ikea, and Nike—along with countless smaller companies—have made changes to increase the sustainability and transparency of their supply chains, which has helped to popularize and engrain monikers like "fair trade," "organic," "local," and "sustainably sourced." There are even multiple stock indexes that chart corporate sustainability, including the Dow Jones

PEOPLE, PLANET, PROSPERITY

Sustainability Indexes, MSCI Global Sustainability, FTSE4GOOD Index, and the Ethibel Sustainability Index.

Both consumers and policymakers are now focusing as much on rewarding sustainability innovation as they are on punishing polluters. "Carrots are better than sticks," one energy policy consultant told me. This shift goes beyond just environmental sustainability. "What we discovered about corporate risk," Rod Robinson of ConnXus told me, "from legal risks to long-term financial risks and viability, is that things like racial discrimination or even slave labor in your supply chain damages public perception." Many companies are becoming socially responsible simply because it makes financial sense. What is also encouraging about this is that we are seeing a flurry of growth in businesses that are owned and staffed by people of color and companies that want to offer living-wage jobs in the developing world.

Companies that try to hide nefarious business practices are now facing the wrath of a more informed public. Just in the last few years, protests have been successful in changing the social and environmental policies of Johnson & Johnson, Fruit of the Loom, Nestlé, and Staples. Shareholder revolts rocked mining company Rio Tinto over its coal lobbying push in Australia, and Royal Dutch Shell was goaded by shareholders to align its emissions targets with those of the Paris Climate Agreement.

Generally, this push for "Corporate Social Responsibility" promotes companies that generate broad public benefit (employee health, environmental sustainability, community prosperity, etc.) aside from financial profits. Until recently, companies were legally obligated to pursue profit for their investors. This "shareholder primacy" prevents businesses from prioritizing the social good over financial returns.

Incorporating as a "public-benefit corporation" or "B Corp," as opposed to a "C Corp," expands an enterprise's legal charter to include actions that focus on the social good. The non-profit B Lab, which created the "B Corp" legal status, also developed a certification that assesses companies by their supply chain, internal governance, employees, and overall social and environmental impact. There are over 3,500 certified "B Corps" including Patagonia, Ben & Jerry's, Method, Nutiva, and Alter Eco.

Yet beyond any impressive monikers, many companies have strong social-equity or environmental thrusts simply because it is a passion of their leaders. Akola of Dallas, Texas, is one such company. I spoke with Akola COO, Brennan Lowery, about her company's mission and modus operandi.

"We are a jewelry manufacturer and retailer that trains and employs women in crisis in Dallas, Texas and East Africa. We help women from a huge range of backgrounds: formerly incarcerated women, illiterate women, those without formal education, or simply women without credit or financial options. Many start out working in our jewelry-production facilities, then we encourage their upward mobility to our retail outlets, distribution center, and our main office."

Brennan explained how she balances the company's financial and social goals. "The financial bottom line certainly matters, but maybe even more, we measure success by how many small businesses our women start with the money they earn from working for Akola.

"Many also go on to buy property or land, which is a huge leap, especially in Uganda, where most women start out as illiterate and without much social power. As a COO, I like to grow our business, but it gives me deep, lasting joy to see women grow in confidence as they develop the skills to take back control of their lives."

I asked Brennan what she would say to a business owner or CEO that may be considering taking their company in a socially positive direction. "I always say that CEOs have a responsibility to have goals that are bigger and broader than just their bottom lines. So I certainly support other leaders moving in that direction. But to avoid feeling overwhelmed, my advice to them is not to try to make sweeping change all at once. Pick a facet of the company and add a socially responsible aspect to it. See how that goes, then add other similar elements in other parts of the company and let it grow into something inspiring."

Social and environmental responsibility can eventually become part of a company's DNA. Businesses can go beyond simply accounting for their negative externalities, and build positive impacts into their operations. Back in Alter Eco's San Francisco office, Mathieu mentioned something called carbon "insetting." He said that his company completely offsets its carbon footprint from within its supply chains by working with their farmers in Peru to plant trees. It's called "insetting" rather than "offsetting," because the entire business operation is carbon neutral within and of itself.

The topic piqued my curiosity, so I reached out to Daren Howarth of C-Level in the UK. In 2001, Daren invented and popularized the term "carbon footprint," and since then his company, C-Level, has created something called "carbon balancing" which makes carbon more about relationships than statistics.

Daren told me, "Rather than purchasing carbon offsets from some distant anonymous place, carbon insetting counter-balances a company's carbon emissions from within its own supply chain. But we take it a step further. We establish direct, personal relationships between a polluting company and the developing-world community that grows the actual trees that offset their carbon."

This intimacy makes these relationships last longer and produces much better results for both the communities and these companies, "including intangible results," he said, "like feeling fulfilled, connected, and purposeful. We actually call what we do 'carbon balancing' because we take the community, local biodiversity, and of course carbon offsetting all into consideration. It's a more holistic, and therefore a more durable model, because when funders know these communities personally, they are much less likely to suspend funding.

Near the end of my conversation with Daren, he told me about his "Aha" moment. Just after graduating from university, he was working in the primordial Danam valley of Borneo as an ecology researcher. He commented to a Malaysian government official about how wonderful it was that the forest had been protected in a preserve. "Yeah, until we need the trees," said the official.

Daren suddenly realized that no matter how much ecological knowledge he had, he couldn't protect the trees from the powerful economic forces that were bearing down upon this region. Soon after that, he was diagnosed with malaria, which in reality turned out to be leptospirosis, a disease he caught by ingesting rat urine while swimming in a tropical river. For weeks he languished in the forest on the brink of death with one faithful caregiver, too weak to travel to a medical facility.

"When I realized I was going to live," Daren told me, "I had an epiphany: I'm not going to waste any time. I felt a massive impatience to cultivate change. I went straight to the source: the business world. I convinced massive companies like KPMG and Deloitte to incorporate ecosystems thinking into their business models. A few years later, my company, C-Level, was born."

Mathieu, Rod, Brennan, and Daren show us that when companies devote significant attention to positive social and ecological outcomes, they not only survive, but flourish. As Mathieu put it:

"What makes me encouraged is what I see in the next generation. They don't accept things at face value. They are much more apt to dig until they find the truth, until they create transparency. This is a global movement toward sustainability and social responsibility in all markets. My message to large companies is that they should get on the sustainability bandwagon now. The new generation of aware, conscious consumers are shifting market demand quickly, and large, inflexible supply chains and production models are being left behind."

The voices in these last few chapters show how business and industry might *not* destroy the planet, and instead enhance it. It's an economy that seeks to empower people rather than exploit them, recirculate materials rather than send them straight to the dump, and regenerate ecologies instead of ravage them.

In the next section, we'll see how our products, buildings, and businesses are shaped into cities. We'll look at how the larger underlying design influences the use of resources, health of economies, and sense of community.

## KEEP EXPLORING

- *What kinds of organizations and businesses do I want my purchases to support?*

- *How would I change what I buy if I knew it had a positive impact on the lives of people who make it?*

# PART THREE

# Cities

———

"WHEN YOU LOOK AT A CITY, IT'S LIKE
READING THE HOPES, ASPIRATIONS AND
PRIDE OF EVERYONE WHO BUILT IT."

—HUGH NEWELL JACOBSON

THE WORST TRAFFIC JAM I'VE EVER BEEN IN WAS ON THE "25 DE ABRIL" bridge over the Tagus river in Lisbon, Portugal. Thirteen lanes converged into three, funneling cars into a narrow span that served as a main entrance to the city. It took me over six hours to go about five miles. At one point, I tried to pass a truck by squeezing into the shoulder on the edge of the bridge. But the driver swerved, pinning me, steel-on-steel, against the side rail, inches from falling into the river below. I don't know which was worse, the terror of that encounter, or the drudgery of four more hours of traffic that followed.

Having grown up in Los Angeles, the city with perhaps the most notorious traffic in the US, I was no stranger to bumper-to-bumper transit. Trevor sometimes complained about his San Francisco Bay Area commute, but I had to remind him that traffic was ingrained in the culture of my upbringing. Saturday Night Live's "The Californians" is a skit entirely centered around people in LA talking in caricatured surfer accents about which routes are best for avoiding traffic—and it's not that far from the truth. The dreaded 405 freeway gobbled up more of my afternoons than I'd like to remember. Over the course of a day, half a million cars pass through the interchange between the 405 and 10 freeways, making it one of the busiest intersections on Earth. It's such an infamous freeway that I often saw homages to it on license plates. My personal favorite was "H8N D405."

It wasn't always like this. For decades, LA had an extensive light-rail commuter system, known as the Pacific Electric. However, in the 1950s, a conglomerate of oil and tire companies bought out and dismantled the entire system—as they did in 60 other metro areas in the US—in order to ensure our need for the internal combustion engine.

And it worked. Most major metro areas are largely dependent on automobiles and a spider-web-like network of freeways. Their biggest victory is that the majority of US urban residents must rely on the car as the only option for getting around. In many places, city planning has become synonymous with simply managing the flow of traffic and the never-ending need for more lanes.

It feels intuitive that more lanes mean less traffic. As long as we expand the road to keep pace with a growing population, we'll be fine. That's exactly the logic used by engineers to build out trillions of dollars in road-widening projects over 70 years. Why then does traffic keep getting worse?

The reason that adding lanes doesn't solve the problem, and why most expansions typically lead to the same amount of congestion, has nothing to do with the size of the road. The issue, rather, is one of perception.

Donald Shoup coined the term "induced demand" to describe this phenomenon. Essentially, when we add lanes to a road, we make it more inviting to drive. People who otherwise would have taken an alternate route, hopped on a bus, or found a job elsewhere now pile onto this newly widened stretch of pavement. Sociologist Lewis Mumford once quipped that curing congestion by adding more lanes is like curing obesity by buying bigger pants.

If adding more lanes doesn't do the trick, then what *do* we do? Is resisting traffic futile? Are we doomed to a future of ever more gridlock?

When we scratch below the surface, we find that traffic isn't the problem we should be solving. It's a symptom brought on by something much deeper and more fundamental to how we've laid out our cities. The question we should be asking isn't how do we reduce congestion, but why is everything so far apart? Why is the nearest grocery store a ten-minute drive? Why do I work 20 miles away from home? Why can't I walk to anything?

One reason is that, in many areas, it's been made illegal, through zoning, to live close to the places we work and the things we like to do. We've separated and concentrated the different parts of our cities with such intensity that we now must drive to everything.

It wasn't always this way. When early American cities were laid out, neighborhoods were normally a mix of housing, shops, and light industry. The vast majority of urban areas built in the 18th and 19th centuries have this overlapping mixed-use plan, the center of which is often referred to as "the walkable city." But around the turn of the 20th century, something changed. Pollution, overcrowding, and poor sanitation in the core of industrial cities made residents long for the greenery and space of the countryside. This pastoral ideal was empowered by the automobile. People could now live outside the city and commute downtown.

The shift to suburbanization was dramatically accelerated by the Allied victory in World War II. Veterans returning from the war needed homes, so the Federal Housing Authority and Veterans Administration subsidized an explosion in construction by granting millions of mortgages. These benefits were limited primarily to white folks, as the racist policy of red-lining made it very difficult for Black Americans to get loans to buy their own homes, especially in certain neighborhoods. This policy deepened segregation and discrimination in the surburban world that was taking shape.

With interstate highway legislation in the mid-1950s, the focus of city-building shifted from placemaking to distance and speed. Multi-lane highways were constructed to accelerate suburbanization and, among other reasons, to allow for emergency evacuations in the event of a nuclear attack. Plowing through hinterlands, the government paved escape routes from cities and made it much easier to live farther away.

New technology and security concerns were combined with a philosophy that favored the logic of the factory. Modernist planners re-envisioned cities as machines where each zone had a unique function in an efficient whole. They divided the places we live, work, and play—separating them from each other by vast distances. Neighborhoods were master-planned and tract homes were pumped out like products on an assembly line. Today, suburbs comprise endless stretches of single-family homes branching off extra-wide arteries, connecting us to long strips of titanic-sized stores and office parks miles away from where we live. Like baseball, apple pie, and jazz, suburbs and highways quickly became iconically American.

One of the greatest casualties of this type of development is that we as the residents have been removed from town-building. The residents' vision for the places they live has been replaced by those of large developers, retailers, and engineers. The result has disconnected us from the true cost of development. It's led to a highly subsidized system where every year state, local, and federal governments spend more to make parking "free" than the entire country spends on Medicare. As we'll see in the following chapter, the way we've woven wood, metal, and concrete into urban fabric costs much more to maintain than the money we can raise to keep it from falling apart.

This section of the book is not about how new technologies can improve the impact of our urban world on the planet. It's about a return to traditional town planning that draws from the strength of resilient natural systems and casts aside resource-heavy patterns of modern city making. Ultimately, it's about how people are bringing the things they like, love, and need within walking distance of the places they live. Their stories show how designing cities around walking—rather than traffic—is better for our environment, economy, and quality of life. Many of the people featured in this section are not city planners, but ordinary residents working to revitalize their own neighborhoods. In the future they're building, we may come to spend less time in traffic, and more time enjoying the people and places we love.

# PONZI SCHEME

W E MIGHT LOOK AT BIG-BOX STORES AND SIX-LANE MAIN STREETS and conclude that towns and suburbs are built this way because it gives us the best possible outcome for our economy. The "everything" stores and McMansions of the world must have been carefully optimized over decades to create robust growth at the lowest possible cost to the city, developer, and people.

But when we look at the numbers behind the facades, a different picture emerges. What's often referred to as "sprawl" is not only environmentally unsustainable—modern suburbs tend to produce twice the carbon emissions per person as urban neighborhoods—it's also one of the least *financially* sustainable ways to build a city. We may not see it on the balance sheets of the major developers left standing, but we find it hiding in city budgets all across America. We find it in miles of empty parking lots and declining malls. We find it in failing water systems and bridges, decades overdue for repairs.

US infrastructure continues to receive a grade of D+ from the American Society of Civil Engineers (ASCE). They estimate that the country needs to invest $2.2 trillion over the next ten years to make critical improvements to everything from bridges and roads to water systems and dams. According to ASCE, these upgrades will save Americans $1 trillion. But why would we get so little back for our money? This potential benefit is a loss of over half on their proposed investment.

The truth is that we've built our world in one of the most expensive ways possible. It's caused the US model of city growth to look a lot like a Ponzi scheme, in which an initial illusion of prosperity hides a long-term decline. The only remedy is more investment and growth to maintain that illusion.

Joe Minicozzi, a city-tax expert and urban planner, crisscrosses the country revealing what's been called the "municipal Ponzi scheme" to planners and public officials.

In one of his signature presentations at The Congress for the New Urbanism, he set up a face-off. It was a battle of two buildings. He paired the Walmart in his hometown of Asheville, North Carolina with a building downtown. Looking at the stats of these two properties, we might conclude that Walmart gives us more tax revenue and creates more jobs. We'd be right. A corporate pitch to city council members with the power to approve such projects might make this point.

But when we do the math and look at the revenue of each building *per acre*, we see a very different story. Walmart weighs in at 34 acres and generates $6,500 in property taxes per acre and a respectable $47,500 in retail taxes per acre.

Now let's see how the downtown building stacks up. This little building is one story of retail and five stories of apartments, and sits on one-fifth of an acre. When we do the math, we see it generates $650,000 in property taxes per acre and $86,660 in retail taxes per acre.

Now, what about jobs? The Asheville Walmar t creates six jobs per acre. The downtown storefront generates 73, while also providing housing for 90 people per acre. We might point out that the downtown building isn't even on a full acre, so it's not really creating 73 jobs, while the Walmart *does* create 200 jobs. It's a valid point of course, until considering that a group of similar-sized downtown buildings provide the same number of jobs in under three acres. That's ten times less space than is taken up by the Walmart.

On a per-acre basis, the downtown building provides the city with 97 times the property tax revenue, one and three-quarter times the retail taxes, 12 times the jobs, and infinitely more homes. Concluding that a store like Walmart is better for our economy is like saying your six-foot-six cousin is a better boxer than Manny Pacquiao because he's bigger.

We're talking on a per-acre basis because it determines the other half of the budget equation—cost. The miles of pavement, sewer pipes, and copper wire needed to make Walmart functional dwarf what's needed for a main-street building. The road repairs and trenchings, the fixing of faulty wires—all that adds up to make the cost of a giant building on the edge of town incredibly expensive for cities to support. In one representative example, from 1949 to 2015, the city of Lafayette, Louisiana increased their water and sewer pipes from five to 50 feet per resident. In this case, new city growth required nearly ten times the infrastructure to support the same population. When an acre of land costs more for the city to maintain than it generates in tax revenue, that's where deficits begin to grow.

It's why we've neglected replacing old pipes that leach lead into our water to the point that a quarter of Americans have tap water that's unsafe to drink. It's why our cities are forced to lobby an already broke federal government for trillions of dollars to make sure our bridges and tunnels don't collapse.

By separating and concentrating the parts of our towns and cities like functional sections of a factory, we've been forced to build much more infrastructure than we can afford to support. We've expected small towns to maintain massive shopping centers far from the people who frequent them, while many of our cost-effective, walkable main streets have been left to decay or turned into thoroughfares. Ironically, in many cases, the property tax revenues from these neglected, or so called "blighted" downtown neighborhoods, end up subsidizing the expensive maintenance of wealthier suburbs on the edge of the city. As the power structure of cities tends to favor investment in the more affluent areas, poorer neighborhoods are left with potholes and broken sidewalks. Yet the residents there have paid enough in taxes to fix them many times over.

Chuck Marohn was a civil engineer who used to design the massive roads and pipes needed to enable this form of development. He often found himself advocating for infrastructure that towns and cities couldn't afford.

It was by actually digging into the numbers that he realized what he was doing. One of the first places he looked was in his own neighborhood. He lived in a single-family home at the end of a cul-de-sac. To recoup the cost of paving their street, he calculated that the city would need 37 years of property tax revenue. "That was longer than the road was going to last. It was a dead-end road; we were the only ones who used it. If my taxes weren't enough to cover the initial construction costs, who was ever going to pay to fix it?" He went on to research a wide range of neighborhoods across the country. "I could not find one that came close to covering its own basic expenses."

In 2008, he started writing about it. Since then, his once-small personal blog known as Strong Towns has evolved into a grassroots movement to restore vibrant main streets and economic sustainability across American towns and cities. Today, his organization works to end the growth Ponzi scheme and revive traditional town planning across the country.

To call attention to how overbuilt our cities are, Chuck used to do something hardcore. Back when "planking" was a popular meme he would lie flat on a deserted road in the middle of town and pose for a photo. He dubbed this seemingly suicidal act "stroading." It showed how even though we're still stuck in traffic during rush hour, most of the time our wide roads are empty.

He coined the term "stroad." A "stroad" is a street-road hybrid that combines the worst of both. It's the five-lane boulevard with two lanes on each side and a turn lane in the center. It cuts through most of our towns and cities. It's become the modern-day *Main Street U.S.A.*, surrounded by strip malls and condo complexes.

Chuck clarified what he means by a "road" and a "street." A "road" moves people quickly and efficiently between two points. It's an offshoot of the railroad. A "street," on the other hand, is "a platform for building wealth."

The stroad tries to do both of these things at the same time, and it does them poorly. It tries to carry people as quickly as possible, while constantly allowing cars to enter and exit at the same time. This design defeats the goal of moving people efficiently and is prone to congestion and high-speed collisions.

It also plays the role of main street. Unfortunately, it's hard to window-shop at 40 miles per hour. Streets are meant to provide a place for local businesses to grow. After lunch, we might stroll down to the hardware store or pop into a clothing shop. They provide free advertising through window displays and outdoor signs. A good street invites us to walk just for the sake of walking down it. Maybe we discover a new place that we never would have if we simply punched our destination into the GPS, pulled into a parking lot, and walked into a big-box store.

In essence, the stroad represents the peak of designing around stuff, rather than around people. The result can be disastrous. Chuck pointed out that running a stroad through the middle of town destroys a place's ability to build wealth and support itself financially. You lose the freedom to bike, walk, and have a home near all the things you like to do. "All of that gets simplified down to 'Can you drive and can you park?'"

But rather than shiny new projects to revitalize the walkability of our cities, Strong Towns advocates for first observing where people and neighborhoods struggle. In his hometown of Brainerd, Minnesota, he referenced an experience talking to a mother without a car. She had to push her stroller through a ditch because there was no sidewalk to get where she needed to go. According to Chuck, city investments in walkability should be prioritized to respond to needs like these, and build incrementally off effective projects.

Strong Towns works with cities of all sizes, improving main streets across the country. They seek a return to sustainability both environmental and economic that's rooted in the physical design of our places. It doesn't require new technology and is something our ancestors before the automobile understood. It's a return to letting neighborhoods evolve around the unique lives of their people, rather than the 20th-century approach of building them all at once. The goal is to restore our ability to maintain what we've built by bringing the scale of development down to a level where ordinary people can participate.

## KEEP EXPLORING

- *What is it like walking down the main streets in my community?*

- *How far away are the places where most people live in my town from the things they like to do?*

- *How are people without a car in my community limited from accessing the things they need?*

# GUERILLA TACTICS
# AND THE MASTER PLAN

THERE ARE TWO PATHS TO REVIVING THE AMERICAN MAIN STREET. One is small-scale, scrappy, and immediate. It's best for converting over-wide thoroughfares back into the destinations they once were, before the flow of traffic became all that mattered. The second approach is master-planned, well-funded, and slow. It's goal is to remake places that intentionally limited our walking to a narrow path from car door to front door. It's an attempt to raze and then refashion dying malls and their deserted parking lots into walkable blocks.

The first way resembles guerilla tactics and is known as "tactical urbanism." It's often a bottom-up effort, led not by city administrators or urban designers, but ordinary citizens with a vision for what their neighborhood could be. While these quick-and-dirty projects may seem inconsequential on the surface, they have the potential to revitalize the wealth and walkability of entire neighborhoods and inspire many others to do the same.

Jason Roberts loved his Dallas neighborhood, but he felt something was missing. He recalled stories from his parents about what Oak Cliff used to be like when they were growing up. "I would hear about the little main streets they'd have with the parades, and everybody knew the local pharmacist and the local cafeteria owner. Everybody looked out for the kids and they were all friends." He spoke with nostalgia for the sense of community that used to exist in American towns. "I didn't have anything like this," he lamented. "There was no pride in the place and there was a lot of frustration from folks in my community that we really had nothing to celebrate in our neighborhoods."

He would spend several years looking for inspiration from American cities. He saw how activists in San Francisco had remade parking spaces into little parks. They'd set up places to hang out right on the street by using a loophole: as long as you feed the meter, there's no law requiring that you use the space for parking your car. These park(ing) days led to the permanent creation of parklets that provide areas to sit and enjoy the space where cars used to be. He looked at the redesigned streets and bike lanes of Portland. He looked at the work of Janette Sadik-Khan, transit commissioner in New York City, who converted the busy streets and concrete islands of Times Square into a park-like urban plaza.

He took all those ideas for building vibrant places and presented them at City Hall in his hometown. "I found that when you're the person who shows up at City Hall and says those things, you'll see a lot of people who will come out and say, 'No! Absolutely not! You're not going to cut our roads in half. You're not going to change life as we know it because it's going to be 'Carmageddon.' Business is going to slow to a crawl. I won't be able to drive everywhere.'" Very quickly, he realized that he'd never be able to convince someone who's viscerally opposed to change that the world would be better if we could bike and walk everywhere. He realized that the only way to convince people was to give them a taste of what they were missing.

For that, he took a page out of Janette's playbook. In her mission to make several blocks of Times Square into a walking street, she ran into the same kind of opposition. Her solution: close off traffic for just one weekend. She invested in cheap lawn chairs and asked the parks department to donate temporary planters. For the first time, people were able to experience what Times Square might be like if it were a public plaza. That initial success made it much easier to make those changes permanent.

Jason started with his own neighborhood. He picked just one blighted block—a one-way street with high-speed traffic, narrow sidewalks, and abandoned storefronts. It was a typical block with good bones that had been neglected. It was forced into being a thoroughfare, when deep down it was meant to be a destination.

He studied the local ordinances and found that all the things needed to breathe life back into the street were illegal or burdened with red tape and over-regulation. "Flowers on the sidewalk cost $1,000 in permits. Crowds on the street were actually illegal." It was another $1,000 just to get a permit for café seating. So rather than go through the ordeal of presenting to city council and waiting for a lengthy review, he gathered up a group of people from the community. Together they hatched a plan.

Over the course of a weekend, they'd build the block of their dreams. "We painted our own bike lanes. We added our own café seating. We thinned the streets. We painted murals on the buildings. And we took the empty buildings and put in the businesses we wish we always had." On the windows of the temporary shops, they posted all the laws they were breaking. In an act of self-sabotage, they invited the city staff and the mayor out to see what they were doing. They expected to be arrested. But the opposite happened. When the city government could actually see what the world they were opposing looked like, they realized they'd much rather have it the other way.

"When the city says it's going to take us millions of dollars and years to figure out how to fix this one intersection, we can get some friends together in a few hours." Through the creative use of cheap materials, they made a rough sketch of the town they wanted to live in. "We can take duct tape and realign the street, so that it looks like there's new paint on the ground, so the car lanes get thinner. We can take straw waddles that they use to keep trash out of the gutter during construction and we can make new curbs. And then we can take those wraps that they put on busses as advertising and make new crosswalks."

After the temporary main street had been removed, change came swiftly. The city decided to rewrite parts of their 70-year-old zoning code in a matter of months. Permit costs for outdoor seating dropped from $1,000 to $100.

Today things look very different around the intersection of Tyler and Davis Streets, the site of the event. One of the pop-up shops, an art-supply store, got a lease on the vacant property that they'd used for the weekend. A coffee shop sprang up next door. A Korean restaurant opened up across the street. Now, a continuous stretch of new businesses—bike shop, record store, glasses shop, miscellaneous home decor, clothing shop—line the once-empty strip. The neighborhood was transformed into a place with the street life its residents had imagined.

Following this experience, Jason founded Better Block. This nonprofit helps neighbors form a vision to remake their own streets. In Akron, Ohio, they worked with an alliance of residents to transform a blighted thoroughfare into a Friday-night destination, complete with new music venues. In Ottumwa, Iowa, Jason's organization helped neighbors kickstart a main street renaissance across the state, using the block-building event to train leaders in half a dozen other towns. In total, Better Block has inspired well over 100 projects around the world. What started as a guerilla remake of just a few blocks has grown into a movement embraced by big cities and small towns.

The tweaks to make main streets walkable are relatively cost-effective compared to the changes needed to redesign suburban sprawl. In many of these places, roads are too wide, blocks are too long, and storefronts are too far from the sidewalk to make walking a pleasant activity.

But it may be possible to reimagine the 'burb. Galina Tachieva, Ellen Dunham-Jones, and June Williamson are three titans of what's known as "sprawl repair." They've identified ways to transform dead malls, big-box stores, McMansions, and empty parking lots into walkable town centers. "The good news about sprawl is that it's very repetitive," said Galina in an interview with Chuck Marohn. "There are many principles and larger thinking which can be very much the same in many places."

This revival may begin in the now decaying malls of America. Of the 1,200 shopping complexes in the US, a third of them are dead or dying. In extreme cases, nature has reclaimed these former hubs of consumerism. At the once-thriving Rolling Acres mall in Akron, Ohio, abandoned storefronts are being recarpeted with moss as tree shoots attempt to climb above the escalators. The death of the mall has many drivers in different places, including the rise of online retail and the decline in disposable income from lost manufacturing jobs. But one factor is universal—the fragility of tying business success to big department stores. When for whatever reason they close, their giant spaces aren't easily filled by new tenants. Instead, they can create voids that depress foot traffic to the surrounding stores until the whole complex collapses.

It's in these places that we may transform car-dependent developments into a walkable world for the next generation. For 30 years, Villa Italia commercial center thrived in the middle of Lakewood, Colorado. At its peak, it boasted one-and-a-half million square feet of retail. Then came the fall. Dillard's in the east was the first anchor store to close. Then went Montgomery Ward to the west and JCPenney to the south. Like dominoes, the rest of the stores cleared out one by one, and the crowds changed from shoppers to people "loitering" in what was the only public space in the neighborhood. By 2001, the mall shuttered for good. What remained was a sea of empty asphalt surrounding a colossal L-shaped box.

A year later, the bulldozers came in and flattened the place. A developer bought it for next to nothing. But rather than put up another shopping center with a new veneer, they opted for something different. They converted it into 22 small blocks in order to create the foundation for a new downtown.

The new downtown, known as Belmar, is made up of townhomes, shopping, restaurants, and a public square. The Belmar Square Park hosts events and gatherings. It's where many of the locals come to walk their dogs. Block seven of the 22 is dedicated entirely to artists. On the first Friday of each month, the studios put on an art walk through their galleries. At night, residents can stroll to a number of restaurants and bars in the neighborhood. Previously, Lakewood had no downtown. Today, the new city center is home to thousands of new residents and jobs. In 2013, this revived space generated over four times the tax revenue of the old mall.

It's not just existing developments that can be reimagined. Every year, the urban expanse of America creeps by another two million acres into the countryside. With cheap land, a populace primed for suburban life, and a blank canvas of farms and prairies, the temptation for sprawl is unavoidable.

It was on the outskirts of Gilbert, Arizona, that development was swallowing up farms and spitting them out as new clones of subdivisions. The Johnston Family Farm stood right in this path. When the family heard that neighborhood expansion might claim their last patch of farmland, they got together to find an alternative. If development were inevitable, they wanted to at least preserve the sense of community that exists in rural towns but often gets lost in suburbia. They partnered with a developer to create something different from the neighborhoods around them. "Agritopia" was born from that idea.

They created a residential community, centered around a 12-acre organic farm. Today, grapevines wrap around fences, lining a path that weaves through date palms and fruit trees. Rows of artichokes, tomatoes, carrots, kale, and zucchini grow on either side. During peach season, residents and guests can pick their own fruit, as bees pollinate the crops and make the farm's own honey.

"We believe that it is important to focus on people rather than stuff," read one of their guiding principles from their website. "A simpler life, devoting time to relationships rather than acquiring and maintaining stuff, is a richer life." Agritopia sought a reorientation of suburban values in town planning. They aimed to "eliminate those things that tend to isolate people. Such barriers include: blank walls, overly wide streets, uninviting streetscapes, lack of porches or other social space, garage doors on the streets, lack of usable parks, and speeding traffic."

Shaded porches allow residents to hang out in a space facing the street life. Narrower streets favor walking over driving quickly. They converted the old Johnston farmhouse into Joe's Farm Grill. The bedrooms became the kitchen and the living room became the dining hall. Next door, they built a coffee shop. In a hoop-shaped garage that used to store farm equipment, they created Barnone. It's a workshop space with craft makers including woodworkers, winemakers, a barber, and a brewery. The space includes restaurants, where visitors can dine while perusing the crafts. Agritopia is also home to a school and a senior-living community, seeking to meet the needs of multiple generations.

The development is planning to expand with denser multi-family apartments and retail on the ground floor. They're working to deepen the area's walkability, bringing more activities within close proximity to more residents. Agritopia also advises others who seek to build neighborhoods that combine pleasant, walkable spaces with an active farm.

Ultimately, retrofitting suburbia is an inherently expensive and top-down effort, replacing one master plan with another. Often it ends up creating luxury islands of walkability in a sea of car-dependent sprawl. It's important to balance these efforts with more grassroots, tactical approaches that allow residents, rather than developers, to be the guiding force for change. Sprawl repair may have a place in building walkable blocks where none existed before. Where a main street already exists—and the issue is neglect—it's much more cost effective to focus energy on smaller, tactical tweaks. Moreover, these changes bring neighbors together to create a shared vision for the places they love.

## KEEP EXPLORING

- *Where is the hidden potential among the streets in my community?*

- *How would I reimagine empty parking lots and underperforming malls?*

- *What does the neighborhood of my dreams look like and how might I create a sample of it that people can experience?*

# GROWING ECONOMY
# AROUND COMMUNITY

W HILE SUBURBS CONTINUE TO GROW, FRESH INTEREST AND IN-
vestment have been pouring back into urban neighborhoods.
An Urban Land Institute study estimated that 62 percent of Americans
planning to move in the next five years would prefer to live in places
where they can walk to a mix of housing, retail, and dining. Following this demand, hip new shops, restaurants, and apartments were being fashioned for urban newcomers in walkable places once neglected
by investors. However, the original residents who built communities
through the years of disinvestment were priced out of their own homes.
They were often excluded from the wave of economic opportunity rising
around them.

In 2015, I was one of those newcomers with a relatively high-paying
tech job, living in a low-income neighborhood in South Berkeley. I was
a gentrifier. Though Greg and I eventually moved to different parts of
town, simply changing our addresses did nothing to slow the pace of
displacement. I'd come to realize that the problem has less to do with
individuals choosing to live in specific neighborhoods, and more to do
with the larger trends of urban development.

"The development model we as a society have built is more like strip-mining than gardening," said John Anderson, one leader in a growing movement of bottom-up developers. "You take the money from the place where you've built—what's supposedly urban fabric—and you send that money somewhere else as opposed to recirculating that money within the community."

Outside developers will often buy up large swaths of property. After everything is built and sold, much of the money from the construction, sales, and finance has left the community. If the apartments are owned by a property management company, and the businesses by outside investors, then most of those profits are siphoned elsewhere.

While the development vacuum hovers above, another movement rises from the bottom up. This chapter is not just about improving walkability, but about moving past the top-down economic thinking that enabled car-dependent growth. Creating places around the pedestrian also provides an opportunity to evolve the economy around the community. Through two tales in very different cities, we'll see a new type of real-estate mogul—one who tends to the garden of local wealth.

Monte Anderson (no relation to John Anderson) grew up in Dallas on the south side of the river, "the side of the river where the have-nots lived, or the wrong side of the railroad tracks," as he put it. It was a lower- to lower-middle-income area that experienced a lot of "white flight" in the 1970s and '80s and became a racially mixed neighborhood. "I was one of the guys that stayed and continued to work there even when my friends moved away."

Monte entered real estate through construction, cutting sheetrock for his Dad's contracting company. Eventually, Monte would take on his own development project. He bought a rundown motel with big plans to fix it up all at once. Unfortunately, he couldn't get the financing to renovate the building. Rather than trying to redo the whole thing, he and the staff decided to fix up just one bedroom. Quickly, they saw the occupancy of that room rise to 90 percent, and from there, used the revenue and experience to remake the rest of the motel. Monte realized that success came from pouring love into one little thing at a time and watching it grow.

He found the same to be true in revitalizing a neighborhood. It wasn't about crafting grand plans for redevelopment, but kickstarting the smallest project with the highest impact. Monte began with the smallest thing he could think of—a tent. He started street markets. He started them in neighborhoods where people made just $10,000 a year. He started them in empty strip-mall parking lots and neglected main streets all over town.

"We used it as recycling. Get that junk out of your garage, get that stuff out of your life, get it out here on the street and sell it and make a bit of extra money." He found that even something small like that, with little stands, can have a big impact. "People making $200, $300, or $400 a month extra was a big deal." He went on to use those street markets as a springboard to revive the main streets nearby. At the site of one such market on the farside of Duncanville's neglected main street, he formed a bottom-up planning committee. Together, local residents redesigned their downtown by replacing one lane of road with curbside parking and sidewalk. These simple changes made it easier to access businesses on foot, and kick-started a wave of new storefronts owned by local entrepreneurs.

If most development is like strip-mining, Monte likens his model to farming. Rather than injecting and then extracting wealth, he seeks to grow prosperity from the bottom up. It works like this: 1) "find your farm" (the neighborhood), 2) live in your farm, 3) start a local market, 4) find local entrepreneurs, 5) rent and sell to locals. Repeat.

Monte's projects put a lot of emphasis on live/work spaces. Most are small one-to-three-story buildings with retail or offices on the bottom with residences above or behind. They're incubators for small-business owners, many of whom have never owned their own place. If their business is successful, they can move out of the unit upstairs into a house down the street within walking distance. Now, they can rent out the residence on top to someone else. As he put it, "What built this country is small entrepreneurs owning their buildings with a couple living places on top."

Nurturing these smaller businesses fosters resilience to economic change. When one in 50 local businesses employing ten people goes bankrupt, the impact on the community is much less than if one business employing 500 people goes under or moves out of town. In addition, the smaller main-street buildings are more flexible, easily changing from retail to restaurant to office, and downsizing with a dividing wall or upsizing into one unit. By contrast, big-box stores and office parks do not adapt so easily when their larger tenants leave. Cities can create a stronger economy in the long-term by fostering homegrown entrepreneurs, rather than luring big-name companies with generous tax incentives.

Monte advocates for an *incremental* process of development where the neighborhood evolves bit by bit, rather than all at once. After renovating the motel room by room, he fixed up a dilapidated restaurant next door. In a vacant lot around the corner, he built new homes, one by one, often including extra units for people to run their own businesses. Each new project was designed to strengthen the foundation of what had already been built. The BBQ restaurant was quick to succeed in the space shaped by the refurbished hotel. In the first year, it did $3 million in sales, nearly double what the bank had projected.

After a string of successful projects throughout Dallas that have revived entire main streets, Monte has taken his model across the country. Teaming up with John Anderson and other developers, they formed the Incremental Development Alliance. Their goal is to train 1,000 small developers like them, committed to growing bottom-up wealth in every major city and town in America. Through workshops in lower- to middle-income neighborhoods, they're showing locals how to grow income and create prosperity in their hometowns. Aspiring community developers can learn how to find their farm, clever ways to finance projects, and strategies for hacking local zoning codes to get mixed-use developments approved. The alliance wants to provide essential tools for everyone who walks by an abandoned lot in their community and dreams of something better.

This movement creates a staircase for the dreamers in each neighborhood to make a slow and steady ascent from humble tent to mainstreet revival. And while this path may be an option in some places, in others, the most obvious way up is to move out of town.

For Majora Carter, leaving her neighborhood felt like the only way to succeed. "It was literally on fire when I was growing up," she recalled. "Landlords were torching their own buildings and actually paying people to commit arson to collect insurance money, because that was the only kind of income that was coming in if you owned property." She grew up in the South Bronx during the 1960s and '70s, a period of economic decline, very unlike the idyllic walk-to-work community of the '40s that her father used to describe.

Gentrification takes advantage of all these qualities: the low cost of housing, the walkable urban streets, and the desire of many original residents to leave. "Gentrification begins before you start seeing white people in formerly people-of-color neighborhoods. It starts happening when we start telling the hardworking 'smart' kids that they need to measure success by how far they get away from our communities," she said. "When the time comes where people are looking at our community and going, 'Oh, that's a development opportunity.' We're the first ones to say, 'Sure I'll sell it to you for next to nothing because you must be stupid if you see any value in this.' Where instead they're thinking about the long game, and we're thinking we just need to get out of this place."

Education was Majora's first path out of town, and she went on to pursue a degree at a college out-of-state. But after graduating, it was education that eventually landed her back home. She got into NYU, yet couldn't afford to rent an apartment in Manhattan, and so moved in with her parents in the Bronx.

Her direction in life shifted when the city proposed to build a dump right next to her childhood home. On top of the existing sewage treatment and pelletizing plants already packed into her neighborhood, New York City planned to push another hazard on the community. But rather than driving Majora away, this challenge inspired her. In the time between her studies, she organized a campaign to block the city's plans. After a few years, she and a coalition of local activists won. It was a victory that would spark the beginning of something bigger.

One day, on a stroll with her dog, Majora wandered past an abandoned lot along the waterfront. It sat there with rusty equipment and dilapidated buildings, the ghost of an old bridge project that never came to fruition. Instead of tolls, it collected junk as an illegal dumping ground.

Around this time, she kept getting mailers from the US Forest Service about waterway restoration. "At first, I paid no attention because I didn't realize you could get to the waterfront from our community," she said. "I knew there was a river right by my house called the Bronx River, and I only knew that because I saw it on a subway map, like literally the name of it." But in seeing the empty space by the water, she saw an opportunity to make something better. She applied for the waterway restoration grant from the US Forest Service. To her surprise, she got it.

Before she could come up with any grand plans for what this space might be, she had to make people aware that they had a waterfront. Majora organized open mics and parties down by the river. She brought in a wooden boat-building program where people learned how to make their own canoes. A community coalition began to form around a new vision for the waterfront. They decided to transform it into a park. That old vacant lot would become Hunts Point Riverside Park, the first waterfront park built in the South Bronx in 60 years. The space is now home to grills, picnics, and playgrounds. There's a pier where people can take out canoes and kayaks. Majora even had her wedding there.

With the park's success, she founded Sustainable South Bronx. One of the first things the organization did was ask people what they wanted in their "ideal" community. Often, outside initiatives in low-income neighborhoods prioritize affordable housing projects, community centers, and health clinics. But when residents were surveyed, they listed health clinics and community centers (along with dog poop and litter) as things that made them want to move away.

When asked what they wanted, they listed coffee shops, family restaurants, and parks. "Folks wanted [the] same things that middle-class communities wanted." Most of the existing businesses in the area were fast-food chains, liquor stores, and 99-cent stores. "Instead of finding things like banks and credit unions, you find the payday loan places, the pawn shops, rent-a-centers, those types of things that basically charge you for being poor."

Majora wanted to create places in her community that would make people want to stay. One of her goals was to keep local talent from leaving the neighborhood. "People like to think that brain drain only happens in the developing world. No, it does not. It happens in America's low-status communities of all colors, every single day." One of her first moves was to start a local coffee shop. They founded the Boogie Down Grind Cafe. "We were claiming a bit of coffee culture for us. When people think of specialty coffee, it's like this hipster guy with ironic facial hair and glasses. And I was like 'Excuse me, I'm sorry, but coffee is the Blackest beverage on the planet.'"

Next door to the coffee shop, she launched Startup Box, a company that did quality assurance for tech companies. The idea was to provide an entry into the tech industry for youth in the area. Eventually, her organization would take this one step further, helping to create a place for locals to start their *own* companies. They incubated a locally owned recording studio and eyelash salon. Currently, they're converting a former railway station into an event space and coworking lounge for local entrepreneurs.

She referred to her model of development as "self-gentrification." Though gentrification and displacement typically go hand-in-hand, Majora's model focuses on putting neighborhood prosperity in the hands of the original residents. As she put it, "Why is it that we think that people in low-status communities don't like nice things?" She seeks a way to improve the economic status of a neighborhood through the leadership of long-time residents, rather than outside developers and generally white newcomers.

While Majora's strategy works on a path set forth by the current economic system, there are many visions for change in the Bronx. Some advocate for an alternative to the existing economic order altogether. They focus on community, rather than private ownership of local businesses and property. This model is sometimes referred to as "economic democracy."

One tool of "economic democracy" is the community land trust, a nonprofit that makes property available to long-time residents looking to buy a home. It seeks to decouple land speculation from home ownership, while also allowing residents to build equity. There are many types of community land trusts, but in one common model, you own your home but rent the land from the trust. When you want to sell your house, the trust determines a price that allows you to make money from the sale, while still keeping the residence affordable to locals.

One organization, the Bronx Cooperative Development Initiative (BCDI), seeks to advance economic democracy in the area. They train people in the principles of community ownership and provide an innovation space with high-tech tools like 3D printers and laser cutters for youth to learn the skills of a future economy. They've also launched partnerships to make it easier for local businesses to get contracts with large institutions like hospitals and schools. BCDI and a number of other organizations seek to enrich the community by developing human capital and community ownership.

Whether it's incremental development, self-gentrification, or economic democracy, there's a wellspring of new economic models for urban development. Monte, Majora, and countless others are putting them into practice in neighborhoods across America. Their intention is the same: to reverse the extractive nature of top-down development. Rather than having their wealth siphoned and residents displaced by outside forces, neighborhoods may have the opportunity to pursue a prosperous future from the inside up.

---

## KEEP EXPLORING

- *If local development were driven by my community, what projects would we want?*

- *What can I imagine in abandoned spaces?*

- *What would be the smallest project with the biggest impact in my community?*

# THUNDER VALLEY

'D JUST GOTTEN OFF THE PHONE WITH GREG, WHEN I ROLLED INTO A
gravel parking lot in Porcupine, South Dakota. Here, on the Pine Ridge
Reservation, in one of the poorest counties in America, a powerful form
of placemaking was taking shape.

Andrew "Andy" Ironshell welcomed me at the door. He was the director of communications for Thunder Valley Community Development
Corporation: a non-profit, Native American real-estate developer. They
were working to recover from the trauma of colonization by empowering
local people to reclaim their future.

During our conversation, Andy took out a book filled with pho-
tographs of life on the reservation. "This is the competing narrative,"
he said. "We call it poverty porn." The book, which came out of Aaron
Huey's National Geographic assignment, showed the world images of
life on Pine Ridge. "He got all these great pictures of real life on the reservation. But of course, it shows the harshness."

There is of course, truth to that harshness. Unemployment still hovers around 70 percent. Life expectancy is 48 years for men and 52 years
for women. Many residents live in the equivalent of FEMA trailers with
15 people to a home. Yet statistics and images only tell one side of the
story. Organizations like Thunder Valley reveal another.

The story of Thunder Valley began in a spiritual circle where young members from the community gathered for ceremonies with a local medicine man. "It was pretty powerful that these young people were congregating, looking for themselves, and reconnecting with their traditions, but they would go back home to the same harsh life," said Andy.

In one such ceremony, they were sitting in a sweat lodge, talking about their frustrations with the tribe and all the forces that had wronged them and their ancestors. "They vented 'Oh the tribe should do this, the tribe should do that.'"

It was then that their ancestors answered back. Nick Tilsen, who'd go on to become the executive director of Thunder Valley, was in the sweat lodge that day. He remembered what the spirits said. "How long are you going to let other people decide the future for your children? Are you not warriors? It's time to stop talking and start doing—to not come from a place of fear, but to come from a place of hope."

The message from the world beyond was clear: they had to look inward. In doing so, they'd come to find the talent and power needed for change among themselves. Some were grant writers. Some knew how to organize and speak in public. Others knew carpentry.

Tired of huddling in a small trailer, they decided to focus their first project on creating a new ceremony house because they didn't even have that. As they went about building the ceremony space, their confidence started to grow. "We can do this," Andy recounted. "We don't need experts around us. Together we can figure it out."

They then went searching for ways to carry this message of empowerment beyond their circle. "We didn't want to hand out propane and Pampers every month. That's needed, and we understand how that works, but it's a Band-Aid. It's not systemic change." They spent several years and met with over 3,000 people on the reservation to see what they wanted. Out of those interactions, they developed nine bold initiatives for community empowerment. At the center of it all, they aimed, in the words of Nick Tilsen, to "build an entire 21st century Indigenous community from scratch."

Thunder Valley, the spiritual circle, created Thunder Valley Community Development Corporation. Through fundraising, they were able to buy a 34-acre plot of land along a main thoroughfare, nestled between rolling hills. Renderings of the development showed a mixed-use community with single-family homes, apartments, a community center, retail along the road, a vocational school, and a permaculture farm.

"We're looking at potentially 900 people living here," said Andy. "Right now, Pine Ridge needs 4,000 houses just for us adults. That's not counting all of the kids that are in high school, and 65 percent of the Pine Ridge population is under 25 years old. So there's a huge youth population waiting for housing and jobs and opportunity. We're trying to meet that need."

Their focus is to provide housing across the income spectrum. As Andy put it, "You should be able to live next to the college professor who makes ten times more than you." Though not everyone will be able to live in this smaller community, they want it to be a destination for the surrounding area. "You might not live here, but you get your vegetables and eggs from here, or you might come here to make art."

It's an ambitious plan and not the kind of thing that will go up overnight. "We kind of did it backwards from how the mainstream would do it, where they say 'build it and they will come.' Well, that's a very expensive model if they don't come," said Andy. "Ours is more like, let's build the capacity of the community champions and figure out what they think their needs are, and then support that and build an ecosystem around it."

They started first with a simple straw-bale house. Recruiting students from the local colleges and gathering donated materials, they were able to test what the process might look like. They figured out how to teach young people construction and how to build an energy-efficient house with simple materials. "The process is much more powerful than the deliverables that you see." Rather than relying solely on outside contractors to build their dream, they trained local youth in construction.

When I visited, they were putting the finishing touches on the first seven homes. They were arranged in a circle with an open space in the middle. "Traditionally this is how we used to camp," he said. "We call it *Tiyóspaye*, or family. We really thought about that sense of community in a space. In order to get to the community center, you have to meet your neighbors." The residents of each circle will get to pick what goes in the open space, anything from a garden, playground, or picnic area.

Andy led me into one of the houses. A spacious open-floor plan with a kitchen, dining room, and living room made up the bottom story, with three bedrooms above. It was far different from the current state of housing on Pine Ridge.

According to Andy, the owner of this space was one of the construction trainers who taught the youth who helped build it. He was 24 and had just become the father of a baby. "He's got the 'Dances with Wolves' story," said Andy. "He grew up in a log cabin with dirt floors, no different rooms, just one big space and that's how they grew up. Water outside from the pump. And now he's buying this house."

All the homes were designed to use very little energy from the grid, through tight insulation combined with solar panels. Thunder Valley owns the panels to cover the maintenance, but lets residents reap the benefits of utility savings. It's an important service, as electricity on the reservation can be expensive. Grandmothers often sell handmade quilts on the side while the kids grow weed, just to cover the cost of those bills.

We stepped outside onto the farm. They designed it using permaculture principles with the intention of teaching people on the reservation how to grow their own food. Rows of chokecherries and vegetables were raised next to chickens from a nearby coop. Together the community was regenerating their land as they regenerated their food system. "Ninety-nine percent of the food here is driven in by trucks. So we want to be able to start to feed ourselves."

Andy took me inside the chicken coop. They had about 400 birds, producing over 100 eggs a day that they sold to local supermarkets, schools, or gave away to families in need. At the time, they had just two-and-a-half acres of farmland, but Andy said that once they figured out the system, they aimed to scale it to 100 or 1,000 acres. To do this, they planned to start a cooperative business, Thunder Valley Farms, where the workers will also own a portion of the venture.

When I visited, Thunder Valley employed 65 people year-round. In the summer during their construction training program, that number would shoot up to as many as 100. In a place where people live on as little as $7,000 a year and unemployment hovers around 70 percent, Thunder Valley was creating meaningful job opportunities.

There was a dynamic energy in the office, which was still set up in a portable building. It felt like a cross between a startup and a revolution. A mix of local people from the reservation and others from across America were coming together to make this project a reality.

Yet, Thunder Valley is just one community on Pine Ridge. There are a total of nine political districts, each with their own communities. "We'd like to see one of these in all the districts," said Andy. The development might look different in each place. "We're right along the road here, so retail made a lot of sense. But other more isolated communities might have more agriculture."

They created a template for what a 21st century, regenerative community could look like. It's not meant to be copy-pasted all across America, but to serve as inspiration for how one might go about creating a development process that's reflective of the people in each place.

Since starting Thunder Valley, over 70 other Indigenous communities had reached out to them and expressed an interest in doing something similar. "We don't want Thunder Valley to be the exception," said

Nick. "We had to move beyond inspiration and start trying to build infrastructure and a system that could support a growing movement for Native people." He would go on to found another organization, the *NDN Collective*, to build Indigenous power at a larger scale.

As Nick stepped down from his role as executive director of Thunder Valley, Tatewin Means, who previously served as attorney general for the tribe, stepped up. She has impressive credentials: a degree in environmental engineering from Stanford, a masters in Lakota leadership from the Oglala Lakota College, and a law degree from the University of Minnesota. As an Indigenous woman, she worked hard throughout her life to get to where she is today, but reflected, "You shouldn't have to excel to get fair treatment." Now she works to make it easier for the next generation to thrive. "I want to be a part of that legacy of change and positivity and healing for our communities because that's what's needed. That's what's needed for our future."

Incorporating many voices into a single community vision for the future can be a challenging experience, and at the end of one town-hall meeting, Nick recalled feeling exhausted, ready to go home for the day. But right before he could leave, someone approached him.

"This *unci*, that means 'grandma' in Lakota, she ended up coming up to me. She was 91 years old. And she came up to me and she said, '*Takoja*,' that means 'grandson.' She said, 'That was the best meeting I ever went to.' And I was like, 'Really? Why?'

"And she said, '91 years I lived on this reservation ... But in those 91 years, nobody ever asked me what I wanted for my children's future and my grandchildren's future. Nobody ever asked me those things and meant it. And today, people asked those things to me and they meant it, and I shared them.' And she said, 'That's why this is the best meeting I ever went to.'"

That's the pursuit of Thunder Valley and community builders everywhere. It's a vision for change that asks us what we really want for our future—and means it.

Thunder Valley's strength doesn't come from any one secret sauce or silver bullet, but from the way its leaders have combined many different principles. They've grown incrementally, building off each success to create a time-tested and cost-effective process. They've rooted everything in the desires and culture of the community. They've combined tactical bottom-up action with a long-term vision. And they've bridged the divide between places to live, work, and play, and the land that supports them all.

Remaking our cities to be fit for the future will require us to rethink both physical designs and economic models. Beyond that, it will require us to reconnect what we care about in our cities with how they're built. By coming together as the resident experts, we can begin to create places that future inhabitants may look upon with the same pride and admiration given to the great cities of the world.

As we take this new path, we'll eventually reach the edge of town where neighborhoods give way to open fields and farms. It's here that we move beyond enriching our main streets to enriching the soil that makes them possible.

## KEEP EXPLORING

- *Which individuals or groups in my community have overlooked local knowledge?*

- *What organizations near me are already working to incorporate many local voices into a vision for the future?*

PART FOUR

# Farms

—

"LOOK AFTER THE LAND AND THE LAND
WILL LOOK AFTER YOU, DESTROY THE
LAND AND IT WILL DESTROY YOU."

—ABORIGINAL PROVERB

BOTH OF MY PARENTS WERE RAISED ON FARMS IN NEBRASKA AND farmed into their 20s. As I was growing up, whenever we drove by the high-school gymnasium, my dad would say the same thing. "Hey, Greg, I bet that building could hold a lot of corn."

He never stopped looking at the world through a farmer's eyes. He treated our suburban Los Angeles house lot like a farmstead. He'd often wake me up at the crack of dawn to water and trim the bushes, plant flowers, re-stain the fence, or dig out the occasional tree stump. He didn't want to lose his awareness of the weather, the health of the soil, and the well-being of the family's animals.

When I ask my college students for a show of hands of whose parents are farmers, I get blank stares. About 100 years ago, half of Americans were farmers. Today that number is close to two percent. In the industrialized world, over just a generation or two, we've lost our day-to-day relationship to the land. We've left the open prairies and star-filled nights behind, and now live by the rhythms of traffic, stock markets, nine-to-five schedules, and social media feeds. This one transition could possibly be the biggest underlying cause of climate change. We've largely lost our intimate connection with nature, so we don't feel a need to save it.

"Where does our food come from?" I ask my environmental studies students.

"From the supermarket," is a common response.

When I taught at California State University, Northridge, I'd take my students to work on Tierra Miguel organic farm one day each semester. That field trip was, without fail, the best-attended day of the semester. I attribute this to a core tenet of teaching: students will move heaven and earth (in this case, the latter) for extra credit.

"This is better than a spa day," I remember one student told me, referring to the clean air and palpable silence on the farm. Another said, "I don't even eat carrots, but these are so crisp and light ... I love 'em!" And just-picked organic strawberries, I contend, have no equal.

Working the land, even if only for a day, can reconnect us with our food. We get to feel and smell the soil it's grown in. And on an organic farm, as opposed to conventional farms that use toxic pesticides and fertilizers, you can just pluck anything you see and eat it.

In day-to-day life, it's easy to distance ourselves from the impact that our diet has on the land. When we're so far removed from agriculture it's easier for companies to get away with farming practices that damage the land and degrade ecosystems. In the past, we raised livestock and crops in small-scale, integrated operations that were more mutually enhancing. Today, both livestock and crops are raised in industrial-scale operations that concentrate manure in one place and toxic chemicals in the other.

In the same way that cities were recrafted as metronomic machines cut off from the rhythms of nature, farming has strayed from the logic of natural ecosystems. Industrial agriculture seeks to "surpass" natural productivity via chemical dependence. Many soils have lost their nutrients and now rely on a cocktail of fertilizers, herbicides, pesticides, and fungicides.

A 10,000-acre soybean farm may sit next to a feedlot with 100,000 head of cattle. When separated like production lines on a factory floor, the farm leaches chemical runoff and the feedlot breeds E-coli that flow to the fields downstream. Both operations require expensive chemicals and large volumes of feed or fertilizer to sustain themselves. Half of the grain we grow on the planet is fed to animals, not people. Two-fifths of all land on Earth is devoted to raising livestock. Meat and the way it's produced is draining aquifers, polluting rivers, and degrading the soil. Moreover, most animals raised for food are grown in cramped, miserable concrete food factories, not farms. Most chickens and pigs, for instance, from birth to death never see the sun.

Looking to the model of nature, we find that herds can definitely benefit the fields on which they graze. If herds are managed closer to how they once roamed in the wild, their impact on the land can be one of stewardship rather than destruction. Freed from confinement, pastured animals' manure is scattered more easily and fertilizes soil, while instinctually clustered grazing patterns play the role of gardener for the landscape. When separated into industrial operations, both crops and livestock cause harm, but when joined together they can create mutual benefits.

When we reconnect with the land, even if only for a day of farm work, we're able to see those benefits in action and get a glimpse into the way nature works. We reconnect with something sacred within us, a connection shared between our ancestors and the land on which they learned to survive.

In this section, we visit farms, ranches, and community gardens that heal the land, revitalize our economies, and nourish body and soul.

# SOIL EVAPORATES,
# SOIL GROWS

━━━

I SAW A STRIKING IMAGE ONCE, PROJECTED FULL-SCREEN IN AN AUDITO-
rium. It was at the Slow Money Soil conference, which I attended
while Greg was stuck at home grading midterms. In this presentation,
David Montgomery, an expert on how soil affects the rise and fall of
civilizations, shared a black-and-white photo. It showed what appeared
to be a small hill, on top of which a few cows grazed within a corral.
Surrounding the "hill" was an expanse of farmland with plow marks
running through it.

But this wasn't a hill at all. It was a carving. Over the 60-or-so years
that the family had farmed this land, they'd inadvertently lost several feet
of topsoil. The "hill" was the one place untouched by the plow.

Their farm was a dramatic example of something happening at a fre-
netic pace all over the world. We're losing several pounds of soil per person, per year for everyone on the planet. This isn't something confined
to the last century; it's been going on since the advent of tillage. David
Montgomery pointed out that the survivability and lifespan of all major
civilizations is intimately tied to the rate of soil loss, and often connected
to a time-honored tool of cultivation.

Plows do a number of useful things. They bring up the fertile soil below for next year's planting, kill weeds left over from the harvest, and bury messy crop residue to be reabsorbed by the field. They're a timeless symbol of agriculture, the sculptors of those neat rows featured in Soviet propaganda and model American farms alike. From swords to plowshares and industrial rototillers, the plow is an unshakable archetype of fertility, stability, and healing. But the plow also has an unfortunate secret that's threatening to destroy the very things it represents.

When a plow tills a field, it exposes carbon-rich soil to the air. This soil carbon bonds with oxygen to form $CO_2$, which floats off into the sky. Poof! Just like that, the soil shrinks a bit, lost into thin air.

Most of the damage happens underground with the destruction of an invisible world. Fertile soil, rich in carbon, provides a haven for trillions of beneficial bacteria and fungi that are the best friends and trusted partners of the plants above. Mycorrhizal fungi wrap their tiny spindles around plant roots, forming a symbiotic handshake. Plants send down carbohydrates made from $CO_2$ in the air mixed with hydrogen from the water, and powered by the sun. In exchange, the fungi and specialized bacteria send up key minerals that the plants need to thrive. All of these nutrients make their way back to us on our dinner plates.

The overuse of plows shatter these networks, ripping apart the complex systems of nutrient exchange. Today, farmers in the United States have been able to boost food production by substituting the work of these soil organisms with chemical solutions. But, it's a fix that's come with consequences. Produce has actually lost much of its nutritional value, fertilizer runoff has caused dead zones in the Gulf of Mexico, pesticides are killing everything from bacteria and bees to people, and on top of it all, these chemical inputs aren't cheap. Many farmers are struggling year after year to break even. The age-old tradition of passing family farms on to the next generation is fading, as the youth set their sights on better prospects elsewhere.

Is it possible though to forgo 10,000 years of Western farming tradition, and still feed the modern world? What does it look like *not* to till and spray a field?

At first, it may seem messy or even counterintuitive, as next season's crops get planted among the mowed stems and leaves of last year's harvest. But think for a moment about a forest floor or grass-covered prairie. Do you ever see a wide stretch of bare ground humbling itself so that just one perfect plant can grow? Of course not. The ground in the wilderness is a diverse mix of plants, animals, and microorganisms, both living and dead. We don't think of it as messy or disorganized. We think of it as beautiful—a mysterious combination of life and death that supports a rich community of different creatures in a seemingly eternal balance.

By reducing tillage on a field, the power of that community enters the farm. When the land isn't chopped up, a micro-metropolis is safe to grow and expand, reaching deeper to find precious minerals locked as far as 20 feet down. This universe in miniature is populated by trillions of organisms and built out of carbon.

Concentrating carbon in the soil could have implications for the atmosphere. Rattan Lal, one of the world's leading soil scientists, argued that on a large scale, this process may create a sink for greenhouse gasses. "The total amount of carbon we have lost in the soil throughout the world is 130 gigatons. So how much can we put back? It's about that same amount—130 gigatons. What does that translate into $CO_2$ in the atmosphere? We can draw down about 65 parts per million of carbon dioxide." Even today, the Earth's depleted soils already store more carbon than the atmosphere, all plants, and all animals combined. The potential is massive.

Reducing our reliance on the plow is one way to revive the soil. Another has four legs and four stomachs. Enter cattle. Long labeled by many environmentalists as a scourge on the planet, cattle may be an unlikely partner in this story of recovery. If the bacteria and fungi are the stewards of the deep, then grazing animals may be the ones above.

When cattle are raised in crowded feedlots, they can be quite destructive. Their concentrated feces runs off into rivers, contaminating fresh water and ruining ecosystems and the livelihoods of farmers downstream. In Brazil, international demand for beef pushes ranchers deeper into the Amazon, forcing them to clear-cut ancient forests and leaving deserts in their wake. Deforestation for animal agriculture is now the leading cause of terrestrial species extinction.

It seems cattle can do no right. Many believe it's best to shut down ranches and eliminate beef from our diets altogether. There are, of course, huge environmental and health benefits to eating less beef, but cattle may have something special to offer beyond their meat. What if the problem isn't just the sheer number of them, but how they're raised?

Cattle were domesticated from the Aurochs, a magnificent beast twice the size of the modern bovine. They roamed in herds across Europe and Central Asia, fending off wolves and saber-tooth tigers with their massive horns.

While the Aurochs are no more, their natural behavior of clustering together in tight groups is ingrained in today's cattle. When cattle, like wild bison, are allowed to move together as a herd, nudged from place to place to mimic how they once tried to stay ahead of the wolf pack, something remarkable happens. Instead of picking out the tastiest greens and leaving nothing but bitter weeds to overtake the field, they graze the plants more evenly.

As they move along to greener pastures, they leave behind natural fertilizer. Their four-chambered stomachs take tough cellulose and break it down into calories. What comes out the other end is a carbon-rich mixture, teeming with gut microbes eager to join those below ground. The cow processes grass into a form that can be quickly absorbed by the next generation of plants. And that's exactly what happens.

The grass comes roaring back, stronger and healthier than before. As the cows rotate around the farm or ranch, each patch pulses in green.

The rotation accelerates the buildup of carbon in the soil.

This only works if each patch has ample time to recover, sometimes up to a year. The scenario quickly becomes destructive when large numbers of animals are inserted into a landscape, and left to continuously overgraze the land. But there's evidence that some landscapes may be better off with a few cows managed in a way that mimics wild herds, rather than no cows at all. In order for these beneficial bovines to enhance landscapes in this way, they must leave the massive factory farms and return to their pastoral roots.

Gabe Brown is a North Dakota farmer who, over several decades, has removed the plow and added the cow. In a demonstration, he picked up a big clod of his carbon-rich soil. It was dark, the color of night, and held together as one mass. He placed it in a jar. In another jar was a lump from the farm next door. He took a hose, filled each jar, and walked away. Hours later, he returned.

One jar looked like the cross-section of a puddle. It was pale brown and cloudy. The lump vanished and was now just a suspension of dust. In the other jar was something completely different. The water was clear. You could see right through to a magnified image of the other side. The clod held. It was just as black and whole as before. He reached in and pulled out the dirt clump from his farm. It barely dripped, no more than a sponge.

Which soil would survive a flood? Which one would hold water in a drought?

The soil from his neighbor's farm tells the familiar story of the flash flood. Five inches of April rain hit a bare field. Rather than being a blessing, the downpour carries off dirt in a wash of runny mud. When the storm clears, the farmer discovers half the land has taken off. It's in the river now. Next week, it may be in the Gulf of Mexico.

Now, let's see what happens when the same flash flood hits Gabe's farm. Water seeps through the millions of tiny underground canals excavated by the fungal civilization. It pools into countless microscopic reservoirs. It twists into the deep complex world below—an impressive natural aqueduct system—which is ready to catch it. Above ground, some puddles may form as the soil becomes saturated, but the field holds. In the morning, Gabe finds his fortune intact.

On one farm, these benefits may be personal, but over many they could be profound. As one farmer I spoke with, Gail Fuller, put it, if all farms could fully capture the rain, "You might be able to recharge the Ogallala Aquifer." Instead of flooding towns and fields, the extra water trickles deep into the ground, refilling an ancient reservoir that makes farming possible in many states.

Soil is the beginning and end of life on land. Healthy soil can do the work of expensive chemicals, hold water in times of drought, and restore the ecology of the land. It nourishes the crops that feed the human world, and in the process it stores more carbon than all the planet's forests. If we allow this cradle to thrive, it will return the favor.

---

## KEEP EXPLORING

- *What health benefits would I or my family enjoy by eating more nutrient-rich food from healthy soil?*

- *How can my food purchases support local farms that build, rather than deplete, soil?*

- *How might building the soil make my community more resilient to droughts, floods, and fire?*

# STEWARDS OF THE PRAIRIE

—

UNLIKE GREG, I'D FIRST ASSUMED THAT GROWING HEALTHY SOIL would only be practical on small, organic farms. However, some of the strongest evangelists of good dirt once practiced *conventional* agriculture on thousands of acres. Their shift towards a *regenerative* form of farming comes from the fact that healthy soil, on any scale, can make economic sense. It has allowed many farmers and ranchers to turn net losses into financially sustainable operations. They've rediscovered that the fate of farming, the health of the land, and the economy of the Great Plains are intimately intertwined. Together they're erecting a living infrastructure of fertile ground that, rather than decaying over time, grows stronger with every harvest.

Before he became a farmer, Darin Williams used to build houses. Every morning he'd drive an hour-and-a-half from Waverly, in Eastern Kansas, to Kansas City, Missouri. Though he dreamed of farming in his hometown, the economics just didn't add up. "There was a general sense that you needed to get a job and leave the community to make a living," he said. As farms went out of business and real-estate developers started buying up the land around him, Darin felt like this was the last chance to pursue his dream. "I didn't want to die knowing I didn't get to farm."

It was during this time that he happened to see a presentation by Gabe Brown, the North Dakota farmer who'd used the lessons of nature to create fertility without chemicals. "It just really struck a chord with me. This could be the missing link." Darin would come to realize that the key to wealth on the land lay in stewardship of the soil. He changed his career, and went from building houses to building soil.

First, he started with the foundation. He took a degraded field and covered it in a layer of chicken manure. Those first two years were all about repairing the pasture. Once it was fertile enough to grow food, he introduced a rotation of cover crops and cash crops. Then he brought in cattle, moving them in a way to give the land time to recover. This relationship between nitrogen-fixing cover crops, the protective mulch of crop residue, and the action of grazers sparked life in the soil, while pulling carbon out of the air.

As we drove past one of his fields, I saw tiny green specks poking out from the dense remnants of last year's harvest. With my untrained eyes, I noticed that some of his neighbors had similar green patches, and I assumed they were the same. We pulled up closer to get a better look. The green on the neighboring pastures was pigweed, a nuisance that has to be sprayed with weed killer. To help the desirable crops survive these herbicidal conditions, farmers often turn to seeds that have been genetically modified to resist the poison.

The green of Darin's farm wasn't pigweed. It was volunteer rye that planted itself from seeds that escaped the combine harvester. For essentially no extra cost or passes on the tractor, he'd planted a useful cover crop that would become forage for the cattle and would also take care of the weed problem. Often, once the rye takes root, it outcompetes the weeds that might find opportunity on bare ground.

Darin pulled out a shovel from the back of his truck and planted it in the earth. He lifted it up and showed me the dirt. Its shape resembled a solid chunk of cottage cheese, held together with roots and an invisible glue of microscopic mushrooms. A few earthworms wiggled about and a column of ants marched out of the ground. The land was still healing. Below the first four inches, layered stripes told the story of years of compaction from the plow. We walked ten feet over to a field farmed by his neighbor. Darin dug up the same-sized chunk of dirt. I pinched off a piece and rubbed it between my fingers. It disintegrated into a grainy paste that felt like a cross between the beach and a puddle of mud. This scoop of earth seemed empty. It was a uniform mass with no signs of life.

Life was what made all the difference. In Darin's rejuvenated soil, he was able to grow 46 bushels of soybeans per acre, which was nearly double the country's average of 26. But it wasn't having the highest yield that mattered. He said that farmers had become obsessed with yield as the main measure of success. Indeed, there were other farms in the area with higher yields than his. The difference, however, was marginal. "Their best GMO bean only yielded one bushel better than my best soybean," he said. "That really opened my eyes. I thought, 'What in the world are we doing? Why are we paying Monsanto those fees?'"

What was the cost of squeezing out one more bushel per acre? Farmers had to pay for fertilizer, insecticide, herbicide, and seeds—all of which, when added up, reduced their income. It made more sense to grow slightly less when the cost of doing so was significantly less. Darin didn't worry so much about yield. He was focused on building up carbon in the soil. "Nothing else matters on our farm if we can't get the organic materials."

He wouldn't be able to make ends meet if he only focused on output. "I would have had to get a second job, or go back to building houses, if I'd kept tilling the ground," he said. "People are not profitable doing it that way."

That was not how his neighbors saw it, though. When the farmer next door retired, he made sure Darin never had a chance to buy or lease the property because he didn't want his ground farmed regeneratively. "They think we're crazy," said Darin. "But they haven't been making any money on their farms for the last five or six years, and I have." Darin said he had an arch-enemy in town. "He's an older guy and he can't stand what I do. But he's bankrupt." Darin smiled and pointed at one of his fields. "As a matter of fact, he used to farm this patch here."

Darin's operation, like that of many farms practicing regenerative agriculture, was not certified organic. He still sprayed some chemical fertilizers and the occasional treatment of herbicides, which he described as a "strategic strike" rather than a general application. But he used progressively less with each strengthening of the soil.

"Most people average 400 hours on the sprayer each year. I've put in about 100 hours in four years." According to his claim, he used one-sixteenth the chemical inputs that some of his neighbors did, and he'd reduced his inputs by half from when he started. By not spraying or tilling, he also spent about a third of what his neighbors did on diesel every year, not to mention hundreds of hours of his own labor.

Before I left, we drove down the road, leaving the baby rye behind. We ended up at a sheep farm. The pasture faded from patches of green that grew thinner and thinner, until the ground turned pitch black. Darin said that this overcrowded pasture couldn't support the number of sheep. Sooner or later, he expected this operation to collapse under the weight of its expenses and necrosis of the land. Whatever money the owner might be making was being sucked right out of nature's bounty. It won't last forever. By contrast, the money Darin made came from building nature's bounty. With every season, the soil regenerated a little more.

As farm after farm breathe life into the land, we may forget that before we plowed the plains, these were some of the richest soils on Earth. Reaching back in time, we can learn from the original stewards who first built this fertile ground.

For tens of thousands of years, the prairie was the territory of the buffalo. These sacred stewards tended to the grasses, fertilizing them as they passed. They were walking seed banks, carrying the beginnings of forests in their fur. They were vital to countless nations before the arrival of European settlers, providing food, clothing, shelter, and ceremony. But they were hunted to the brink of extinction.

Regenerative grazing tries to substitute the benefits buffalo once provided by using cattle, sheep, and other livestock. While there's nothing wrong with applying the behavior of the buffalo to heal the land with other species, could it be possible to do the same with *actual* buffalo?

On the far edge of Western Kansas, in what was once Arapaho land, I drove past a gate mounted with a bison skull. On the other side, a man in a leather vest that had turned black along the creases welcomed me with a firm, earnest handshake. We went inside and sat around the dining room table, eating fresh-baked bread that his wife had just pulled out of the oven. She worked as a natural healer in the community. "She helps people with whole-health issues. She does the holistic body stuff, and I've got the land thing," said Ken.

Ken kicked off the conversation with his roots. He grew up in Chicago, but his parents were Serbian immigrants. After World War II, the Soviets purged what would become Yugoslavia of anyone with German ancestry. Ken's family was caught in the crossfire. They left everything behind, including the farm that had been in the family for generations. They barely escaped the death squads that swept through the countryside, and his family sought refuge across the Atlantic.

Ken grew up in the city, but wanted a different kind of life. "I left the day after I graduated high school." He went out west, where he became a backcountry guide. Eventually, he found work as a ranch hand on a 100,000-acre bison ranch that happened to be owned by Japanese billionaires.

The ranch was losing money and, soon after Ken joined, they fired his boss and promoted him to manager. It now fell on Ken to get the finances in order. Out of necessity, he sought a new way to work the land and came across a grazing system developed by Allan Savory in the arid grasslands of Zimbabwe. Savory offered a prescriptive approach to managing all aspects of the ranch, from the movement of a herd to financial health and daily routine. "I applied it on that ranch whole-hog." He changed the way they did things, guiding the bison to mimic how they once roamed in the wild. After a year-and-a-half, financial conditions on the ranch improved. "We started increasing the stocking rate over and over and over. When I left, we had over 3,500 buffalo." The owners were understandably shocked when Ken started cutting them million-dollar checks from a supposedly failing operation.

Even more astonishing was the effect these new practices had on the local wildlife. When Ken began, there were 70 wild elk living on the ranch. "By the time I left, we had 700. They were voting with their feet and decided it was better to stay on the ranch than to go up into the mountains because the grass was so much better." Today that ranch is owned and stewarded by the Nature Conservancy.

When it came time to renegotiate his contract, Ken got smart. He asked for a herd of buffalo and some land to start his own operation. That land became the Homestead Ranch.

Ken's story reads like a bizarre mashup of the American dream—a son of German refugees who worked his way up to a homestead on the prairie by bringing back the buffalo for Japanese billionaires. It got him where he is today.

At first, however, it seemed like nature was conspiring to cut his journey short. The year Ken started his ranch was the beginning of one of the worst droughts in the region's history. "We've been in a drought for the entire time. This is worse than the drought in the '30s, in the dust bowl. As a matter of fact, this has been compared to the drought that made the Anasazi civilization collapse."

Many of his neighbors have not fared so well. While farmers have been able to survive on crop insurance payments from the federal government, ranchers don't have the same safety net, and many have gone out of business. "We don't take any payments at all. Our safety nets are built into our business model," he said. As nearby ranches fell into bankruptcy, Ken's operation went the other way. "We grew this ranch and expanded this ranch, and did it profitably in the worst weather patterns possible."

In the summertime, you can see why the Homestead Ranch has thrived through year after year of drought. "You drive down one of these county roads when they're farming. *Boom!* You've got these hot winds blowing and it's just a blast furnace coming off those fields. And you go to where there's a corner of grass, like our grass, and it's 15 to 20 degrees cooler." Without bare ground, the grassland that the buffalo built acts as natural air-conditioning, keeping precious water from evaporating. It's benefits like these that can help us grow food in a warming world of unpredictable weather.

Working with nature is the secret to Ken's success. From the way he moves bison to the way he thinks about the true wealth of the ranch, he seeks to follow nature's rules. "We're not mining the soil, we're regenerating it ... making it better for the next generation, and that is real wealth, real stability, and real health." He doesn't pay for pesticides, herbicides, fertilizer, or feed because the buffalo have revived the soil to provide those services over the last 20 years. This practice has allowed him to create abundance in a time of supposed scarcity.

Ken wanted to show me what that success looks like. We hopped onto an off-road utility cart and wound our way through the middle of the buffalo pasture.

"If I were walking through here, would I be attacked?" I asked.

"Probably," he said. "If you come by foot or on horseback, they can get aggressive. These are wild animals. They are not like cattle." Buffalo, according to Ken, can be very unforgiving to management errors. "If a cattle guy has a management error, there's a whole bag of things they can use, like antibiotics and vaccines. Well, those things don't work for bison. If cattle don't get fed, they'll stand at the gate and bawl. Bison get discontent with their place, they'll look on the horizon. They'll leave. But if they're happy—and it's not hard to make them happy if you're a good manager—they're very happy to stay home."

While they take more skill to manage, buffalo are much more self-sufficient. "They calve unassisted. Cattle, you got to take the calves off the cow and wean them. Bison, you don't wean calves, they just do it as they've done for eons." And when it gets cold or a blizzard comes, they don't need to stay in a barn. "They're a remnant of the ice age—cold, snow, that doesn't bother them. When it's 30 below, well, it's probably like the last 400 times they've seen this. They're doing okay."

The buffalo sat comfortably, as I shivered in a late-winter sleet, trying to take notes. We reached the top of a hill and Ken motioned to a barren field on the other side. He'd been experimenting with growing wheat. Normally, bare dirt would be a bad sign, but here it was evidence that the land was alive. After decades of stewardship by the bison, the microbial civilization in the soil absorbed the crop residue before Ken had a chance to replant. On a neighbor's field, withered corn stalks lingered. There wasn't enough life in the ground to receive them. It would seem that buffalo have the power to raise the dead, as they returned the land to its former fertility.

We went back inside to look at ways of extending these benefits beyond the ranch. Ken had been developing a conservation management plan for the National Bison Association, in collaboration with Kirk Gadzia, Donald Beard, and Mimi Hillenbrand. Their plan focused on three areas—the land, the buffalo, and the people. "You can't ignore the people. As good conservationists, you need to be engaged in your communities, engaged in sharing information, and engaged in creating healthy economies."

Ken turned the conversation to his own community. "Our little town here is a dying town," he said. "We only have about three crops around here that the federal government will subsidize, so that's all that's grown. When, in reality, you could grow lettuce and strawberries and potatoes. There could be 150 people like me in this county, all doing something different. The impact on the local community would be huge because we all buy different inputs." As farmers struggled to make ends meet with the same costly inputs, Ken hoped that regenerative agriculture could bring economic diversity to the area.

Near the end of my visit, he pointed to something else in the room. "We got a couple of mammoths on the place here." I took a closer look at a bone. "This is a mammoth femur." Beside it was a smaller bone. "This is a femur off a full-grown buffalo."

As I compared the two, he said something that put our time here as humans into perspective. "When I brought it in here, it smelled like rotting bone for three days." Even though the era of the mammoth seemed forever ago, the bone was relatively fresh. I looked out the window at the field, and my mind conjured a herd of mammoths stomping around with the buffalo—two distant cousins separated by time. Together, they built this land.

We may think of the Hoover Dam or the Golden Gate Bridge as towering feats of engineering. But one of the greatest building projects in history is beneath our feet. An invisible infrastructure of healthy, regenerated soil—part reservoir, part cradle, part carbon sink—may one day stretch across half-a-million square miles, from the desert of Chihuahua to the steppe of Saskatchewan. It's driven by an alliance of people, plants, animals, and the microscopic world we can't quite see. It has the power to heal local ecosystems, revive rural towns, and improve the lives of those who grow our food.

## KEEP EXPLORING

- *How can I support regenerative farming and grazing through how I eat?*

- *How might regenerating the soil regenerate rural economies?*

# WISDOM OF THE FOREST

F AR FROM THE PRAIRIES OF NORTH AMERICA, REGINALDO "REGI" Haslett-Marroquín was on his way to agriculture school. The bus rumbled through the Guatemalan countryside, passing by a Civil War that was hiding in the jungle. With help from his brother-in-law, he pulled together all the supplies he needed for school, including a new pair of boots donated from a friend in the army. He was riding into a new chapter of life.

For Regi, it had been a long journey to this point—one that began with a childhood dream. His family made their living by farming a small plot of corn and beans outside of town. From an early age, he worked the fields with his father and brothers. If the crops failed one season, he went to bed without anything to eat. For weeks, he would have to get by on nothing but lard and tortillas. But on the edge of the farm, he marveled at the surrounding rainforest. He saw how nature provided for countless species without lifting a finger. It became his dream to use this wisdom to grow food for those who go hungry.

He was only a few miles away from school when the bus came to a stop. They'd reached a checkpoint where the army searched for rebels among the civilians. A soldier came aboard and shouted, "Everyone off!"

While the passengers lined up with their hands against the side of the bus, the soldiers went through each bag.

"Whose bag is this?" one of them asked.

Regi saw that it was his and, without thinking, raised his hand. As he tried to explain why he was carrying combat boots, one of the soldiers shoved him to the ground. They kicked him, accusing him of being a deserter or worse, a guerilla. Regi repeated the same story. "I have a telegram from the school. It is a government school. I am not a rebel."

At last, one of the soldiers ordered them to stop. "Maybe you're telling the truth. We're going to turn around and count to ten. When we turn back, we better not see you."

He ran as fast as he could. He was aiming for a cornfield that seemed just out of reach. Each number felt like a second closer to his death. He kept running, hoping to put as much distance as he could between him and the soldiers. He heard them count ten. He dove to the ground. Gunfire erupted. Bullets passed over his head. He scrambled into the cornfield, searching for cover among the stalks. As he ran, he could make out the sound of the bus driving away.

That night, a farmer took him in, cleaned his wounds, and gave him a place to sleep. He awoke to find a few tortillas and enough money for a bus ticket to his school. Regi could have died that day on the road. He could have joined the hundreds of thousands of civilians who just disappeared. But he survived, and with him, so did his dream. He'd dedicate the rest of his life to turning conventional farming on its head.

Regi's vision to access the wisdom of the rainforest stars an unlikely hero. It begins with a chicken. We might think of chickens as birds meant to roam free on an open range. But as Regi pointed out, "The chicken is a jungle bird." They evolved in the rainforests of Southeast Asia, pecking for grubs under the canopy. When Regi designs a food system, he starts with chickens under a canopy of hazelnuts and elderberries. He calls this "tree-range," not "free-range."

The chicken may be a "jungle bird," but that doesn't mean it has to live in the rainforest to be in its natural habitat. Today, Regi farms in a much different place from where he grew up. After graduating from agriculture school, he taught classes at an orphanage that was co-founded by his sister. It was there that he met Amy Haslett. She was a volunteer, teaching dance to the children. They fell in love, and when she moved back to the US, he joined her.

Today, their family farm sits on the prairie in Minnesota. In between rows of hazelnuts, Regi cultivates alleys of grain, vegetables, and other crops that chickens like to eat. As the fowl peck for insects and forage, they fertilize everything. Regi likes to think of their digestive system as a small part in the massive "digestive system of the Earth." Just as the bacteria in our gut help break down our food into nutrients, animals break down nutrients for the entire planet.

He explained it like this. When we take crop residue or food scraps and throw them in a compost heap, they can take up to a year to fully decompose. If we feed that to a chicken or pig, the animal can break everything down into manure in two days. During the night, earthworms can break that down into a form that's basically ready to fertilize a plant. "All of that happens within 48 to 72 hours. And it's magnificent."

With the chicken at the center, Regi is able to produce a wide range of healthy food without any chemical inputs.

But, "we don't produce anything," he declared. What he means is that we should look at a farm not as a production line, but as an energy system. "All nature does is organize that energy in the form of cows and grasses and chickens and carrots and all of the stuff we call food. But we don't produce anything," he said. Nature has many "time-tested ways of organizing things that, on one side, are inedible to us, and [puts] them through a process by which they become edible."

If farmers and ranchers aren't producing anything, then what *are* they doing? "We are energy managers, not laborers," he said. "When we manage energy instead of production, then we get into this space where we win significantly: reduce labor, reduce cost, and reduce stress on the landscape."

By looking at farming as managing the flow of energy, Regi quadrupled the output of hazelnuts inside his tree-range poultry paddocks compared to those outside. He did it using zero inputs, other than manure dropped by the chickens as they roamed. In one flock, he experimented with only having his birds feed on forage and sprouted grain, and in doing so, reduced external grain consumption by 67 percent. "If you could drop that price [of raising chickens] right now, without actually doing anything else, but improving our ecology, would you do it?"

In the energy system of a farm, Regi compared soil to a battery. The more it's fed, the stronger it becomes. "At the end of the day, we are harvesting between 30 and 40 percent of all the energy that was captured," he said. "That means 70 percent of that energy goes back into the system." It's the chicken manure, egg waste, crop residue, and leaf litter that charges the soil battery. Feeding the soil makes it so "your next cycle starts better off. And then the next cycle starts better off ... There is no worse off. There are no diminishing returns."

To capture the most energy, Regi thinks of an acre in three dimensions. "Instead of thinking of an acre as 43,560 square feet, we think of an acre as at least 1,111,200 cubic feet." It includes tree trunks and branches that grow many feet up and roots that reach deep down. All that space is part of the same system working with the plants and animals on the ground.

Regi sees the knowledge of the rainforest as a blueprint to transform the food industry from the bottom up. Seventy-eight percent of the people working in agriculture in the US are actually immigrant laborers. As founder of the Regenerative Agriculture Alliance, Regi is dedicated to building support systems and programming for beginning and transitioning farmers. He trains farm workers and aspiring farmers in his permaculture system. The organization provides an opportunity for those largely left out to become entrepreneurs, and to do so using nature's advantage.

Regi put chickens at the center because of the low barrier to entry. They're much easier to manage than larger animals like pigs, sheep, or cattle and only require a few acres and a coop to keep them safe. He designed the system to work on small plots. He estimated the annual gross income from chickens and nuts on a one-and-a-half acre plot can reach up to $41,000. For a three-acre plot that number was $148,000, depending on how the farmer manages and markets their yield.

The Regenerative Agriculture Alliance is building an interconnected network of farms in the US, Mexico, and Guatemala. Each is designed to fit their unique environments. One of the projects on the ground is the permaculture farm at Thunder Valley. That system combines chickens with native chokecherries and buffalo berries and a mix of veggies. Regi's organization focuses on supporting farmers who heal the land, and its board includes North Dakota farmer Gabe Brown, and Nick Hernandez who runs Makoce Agriculture Services, a food-sovereignty effort on the Pine Ridge Reservation in South Dakota.

"If you're fighting nature, guess what? You lose every single time." But if we tap into the intelligence of how nature uses energy to transform soil, sun, and water into food, "we can not only feed the world many times over, but we can fix the climate many times over and regenerate rural economies all over the world."

As Regi works to uplift farmers in the US, Kofi Boa has started a revolution among smallholder farmers in Ghana. Though only two percent of Americans work in agriculture, farming is still the most common livelihood on Earth. Globally, an estimated two billion people manage plots of only a few acres. Kofi seeks to give these farmers the skills to heal the soil, preserve the forest, and grow their income.

His journey into regenerative agriculture began with a fire. One evening, at the age of 12, Kofi waited for his mother to return home. She was out tending to her cacao farm, the family's only source of income. "Deep in the night, I heard my mother coming home, crying in the darkness of the village." A nearby farmer had set fire to his field, a common technique to prepare it for planting. Unfortunately, the blaze whirled out of control as it swept across the brush and up the cacao trees.

This accident was the result of a practice known as "slash and burn," or swidden, agriculture which for millennia has fertilized fields around the world. A patch of forest is cut and the vegetation is allowed to dry. It's then burned, and the ash serves as fertilizer for future crops. If the forest has enough time to recover, then this practice can be done sustainably. But with many more people alive today than in the past, swidden agriculture can cause rapid deforestation. Sometimes, it burns down the neighbor's farm. In 1983, one of those fires wiped out 90 percent of Ghana's cacao farms.

After that night as a child, and in the hard years that followed, Kofi made a pledge. He turned to his mother and said, "I'm going to spend the rest of my life fighting the use of fire on the farmland." He went searching for existing techniques that didn't require farmers to burn the forest. "I spoke to elders in the village and learned that, rather than use fire, they used to cut vegetation, leave it on the ground for a year, and then come back to plant crops." This technique, known as *proka* in the local Akan language, means "to let rot, in order to bring back." Kofi adapted it to work in a quicker cycle, so that he didn't have to wait an entire year for everything to fully decompose. He planted immediately among the cut vegetation, using it as mulch.

Kofi went on to pursue an education that took him from the top agricultural school in Ghana to the University of Nebraska-Lincoln. He learned how no-till works on some of the biggest and smallest farms in the world, spanning the extremes of high-tech and low-tech operations. He decided to put it all into practice back home in Ghana. Leading a government initiative, he and his team expanded no-till by more than 100 times. Participating farmers nearly doubled their family income, while cutting the time they spent working in the field by half. But despite its success, the government decided to prioritize other initiatives, and funding for the project dried up. The momentum of no-till came to an abrupt halt.

Kofi eventually ended up back in the village where he grew up. There, he started his own program, the Centre for No-till Agriculture. Today, he teaches no-till in a way that matches the tools available to smallholder farmers. He shows how the machete can be used to clear the field, chop up vegetation, and make slits in the ground to plant seeds. Kofi's organization focuses on in-person training. "We work on the premise that hearing is believing, but seeing is the truth."

Their goal is to create a class of skilled no-till advocates in communities across Ghana. "We're able to build a group of local farmers and build them into champion farmers. And unlike government workers, unlike NGO staff that can easily be relocated, most of these people are natives to wherever we find them."

Felicia Yeboah, one farmer who learned no-till through Kofi's program, was able to diversify her family's income. She plants maize, beans, pepper, plantain, cocoyam, and cassava. "I can get lots of returns to care for my household," she said. Meanwhile, because no-till doesn't require as much labor, her kids don't have to spend as much time in the field, which allows them to focus on their education. Two of her children graduated from high school. "I am paying for their education through my farm."

The Centre for No-till Agriculture estimated that conservation agriculture increases the disposable income of farmers by an average of 25 percent in the first two years. Kofi hopes to spread this prosperity to the 500 million farmers across the world practicing swidden agriculture. "It is my dream that the whole of Africa will know how to sustain the productivity of a piece of land."

The wisdom of how the forest regenerates its resources may save the forest, while uplifting smallholder farmers around the world. When put at odds, nature, food security, and income all suffer. When brought together, forest cycles enter farm rotations, rather than farms encroaching on forests. It's a relationship of mutual prosperity, where food becomes abundant, local livelihoods improve, and the surrounding nature can begin to recover.

## KEEP EXPLORING

- *How can I support the farm workers who grow and harvest my food?*

- *What organizations focus on the relationship between the livelihood of farmers and the regeneration of the land?*

# FARM IN THE CITY

FARMS DON'T ONLY EXIST IN THE COUNTRY, AND CITIES AREN'T JUST islands of concrete. The last two decades have seen the largest resurgence of urban farms in the US since the Victory Gardens fed the homefront during World War II. These new oases of healthy food are emerging in places where fresh produce is hard to come by. Small-but-mighty urban farms and markets may begin to fulfill this need, while fundamentally changing the relationship between cities and the nutrients that sustain them.

In Denver, Colorado, Beverly Grant watched the middle-class neighborhood where she grew up slowly turn into a "food desert." At first, the term "food desert" threw her off—that a neighborhood's situation could be summed up in jargon. "That triggered me," she said, but not just in a negative way. It sparked an idea. "I had this epiphany about starting a very unique farmers' market."

Where the food industry failed, she planted seeds for healthy living. She created Mo' Betta Green Marketplace, which today hosts four weekly markets in Denver neighborhoods where grocery stores are scarce or non-existent. Beverly refers to this food landscape as a "food swamp," because people have to wade through a litany of low-quality options.

Her competition is fast-food chains and convenience stores, which boast low prices, quick service, and cheap flavor. Mo Betta' works to beat them in every category.

On price, all her farmers' markets accept SNAP, food-assistance currency, to help make produce more affordable. On quickness, they host two cooking classes a week where people can learn how to make healthy dishes that take less than half an hour to prepare. On taste, Beverly shares that it's all about "finding ways to invite people into that sphere of tasting delicious, fast, affordable food." She makes sure that her recipes are so tasty and nutritious that *there really is no competition*.

She even started her own urban farm, growing heirloom vegetables, which can be four to 25 times higher in nutritional value than conventional produce. "I have developed a seed-to-stomach curriculum. I reach people through taste. If it's not delicious, then it's tough to convert people to eating healthy food."

Beverley's mission extends beyond fresh fruits and veggies to healthy living. Mo' Betta offers tai chi and yoga classes on a donation basis to help promote exercise. If that doesn't work, she turns on the music. People can groove on their own or join in on impromptu square-dancing lessons. "Sometimes when you can't get people to move ... they *will* dance!" It's part of what she calls "community weaving." She reaches people "by finding connection points—tasty food, common activities, local accessible places—where we can deliver healthy food and knowledge."

To reinforce her message of health, she spins powerful, easy-to-remember acronyms out of thin air. "We should all eat food that is Traceable, Organic, Local, and Delicious. Now you've been TOLD." Then she reveals HEAL: "Healthy Eating, Active Living." They're simple, yet meaningful words in her language of food literacy.

Sometimes we find the best new ideas in the past. Beverly ties her passion for growing and sharing healthy food to memories of her grandmother. "She turned her entire backyard into a garden in the 1950s and grew everything that my family ate. She told stories of canning 2,000 or 3,000 jars because that was food for the winter. She also made medicine, dried food, and frozen food. I call those things the lost kitchen secrets of yesterday." Beverly has brought that wisdom back to life throughout the markets in her neighborhood.

Communities that lack access to healthy food are often neglected in ways that extend beyond the food system. Quality education, equal protection under the law, and economic mobility are often left out along with grocery stores. "Our economic crisis, climate crisis, prison pipeline, and health crisis all overlap and intersect," said Haleh Zandi, the co-founder of Planting Justice in Oakland, California. "We work right at that nexus. We are essentially decolonizing our food supply."

Where society fails to provide opportunity for communities, Planting Justice plants the seeds for a meaningful and dignified life. The organization hires "people of color and formerly incarcerated people to build organic gardens and raised beds in food deserts where local residents have little access to fresh, healthy food." Those who gain new skills from this work go on to share them and enrich the lives of others in their community.

Anthony Forrest served 20 years in San Quentin State Prison. After being released, he started working with Planting Justice. Today, he returns to the same prison to help with their garden program. "He's a super-important mentor, leader, and role model," Haleh said, not just for those incarcerated, but at local schools, where he helps young people avoid the prison pipeline altogether.

At one high school, two students took what they learned from Planting Justice and brought it to their own community. They started a gardening program, grew natural medicines, and installed a catchment system to collect rainwater. They became champions of healthy living and sustainability and developed themselves into local leaders.

Looking deep into the intersecting web of local issues, Planting Justice focused on one powerful connection point: food. In the same way that regenerating the soil creates a ripple of benefits across the surrounding environment, so does regenerating one central aspect of a community.

When many seeds are planted, they may grow into enough farms and gardens for the city to sustain itself. While it may be hard to imagine harvesting a significant amount of food on urban land, in some places this phenomenon is becoming a reality.

Detroit, Michigan has an estimated 20 to 40 square miles of vacant land. Taking the high estimate, that's nearly the size of all of San Francisco or Miami. Parts of the city blur the line between rural and urban, with overgrown foliage, expanding bird populations, and even wild boars. In a landscape that's become known as the "urban prairie," 1,000 urban gardens have sprouted. Today, they grow 15 percent of the city's food.

Earthworks Farm is one of them. It sits on 20 city "blots"—the term for a space that's smaller than a block, but larger than a house plot. Earthworks grows fresh fruits and veggies for the Capuchin Soup Kitchen, which serves over 2,000 free meals a day to those in need. This two-and-a-half-acre powerhouse harvests 14,000 pounds of produce every year, and offers farming education to thousands of local residents.

The farm manager, Patrick Crouch, reflected on how Earthworks and other urban farms can change the relationship between the city and the countryside. "From the perspective of the countryside, the city is a parasite," he said, quoting Sir Albert Howard, an innovator of modern organic farming. Nutrients are often sucked from rural soils to feed people in cities. When leftover food scraps end up in landfills, the nutrients never make it back to the field from which they came. Food waste decomposes into heat-trapping methane gas, while faraway farms turn to chemicals to fertilize their fields. The distance between soil and stomach creates a gap in the nutrient cycle. Urban farms seek to resurrect this virtuous loop, bringing the cycle of growing and composting into closer proximity.

Growing food in the city, of course, puts farms closer to certain pollutants, like lead. Patrick strongly recommended testing soil before planting. "Lead levels are the main issue, since lead paint wasn't banned until 1972. The EPA suggests that 400 parts per million of lead in soil is safe for living in residential areas, but lead safety levels for actually growing food on that soil are much lower." Testing is a very important extra step, but there are still many places that are good for growing food, even in cities. "There's a myth that urban soils are completely toxic."

The connection to food, land, and the nutrient cycle is not purely physical, it's also psychological and spiritual. Patrick believes that "bringing farms into urban settings reconnects us to many levels of life that urbanism so effectively cuts us off from. It reconnects us to nature and to a more holistic humanity, which makes it harder to abuse the natural system which we are a part of."

Earthworks is just one two-acre plot in a mosaic of urban farms scattered throughout abandoned lots in nearly every city in the US. One study published in *Environmental Research Letters* estimated that the average American city would only have to dedicate about ten percent of its land to grow all the veggies needed for its inhabitants. Much of that may fit seamlessly into abandoned lots and rooftops. Another study indicated that rooftop gardens can also provide cities with natural air-conditioning, reducing interior temperatures on hot days by up to 20 degrees Fahrenheit.

Urban farms are greening the city, as they connect communities with the land beneath the pavement. They challenge preconceptions of where a farm can be and what it can do. It's a place not just for growing food, but for growing skills, leadership, and healthy spaces. Moreover, as the wave of urban agriculture brings the farm into the city, it may simultaneously draw a new generation back to the countryside, inspired to join in reviving the soil and healing the land.

## KEEP EXPLORING

- *How can I access or support nearby urban farms and farmers' markets?*

- *If I could, what would I grow at home?*

- *If my community had its own food garden, where might it be located?*

# BACK TO THE LAND

—

THERE'S A NEW GENERATION EAGER TO HEAL THE LAND. BUT, THEY'RE often separated from the field by a million-dollar fence. Farmland can be prohibitively expensive for young people, especially as many enter the workforce with college debt. The low and often uncertain earnings from working the land, combined with the highly skilled labor required, can quickly turn 100 young farmers into one. With a wave of older farmers preparing to retire, reviving the soil hinges on making agriculture a real career for the next generation.

Near the end of a dusty road in Eastern Iowa, a few patches of prairie are opening up. It was here that Suzan Erem and Paul Durrenburger poured their life savings into a dream.

Their story is a love story. Suzan was a journalist and union organizer. Paul was a professor of anthropology. They met, fell in love, and raised a daughter together. When it came time to retire, they bought some land on a little hill in Iowa, built a house, and planted an orchard. Every summer, they hosted volunteers who exchanged a few hours a day of farm work for room and board. Many aspiring farmers came through, brimming with a passion to grow healthy food and leave the land better than they found it. But they often became disillusioned with the barrier of buying property and the precariousness of short-term leases that don't take into account the timeframe needed to build soil.

Suzan and Paul could have sighed, shrugged, and enjoyed the rest of their retirement, but that's not what happened. Suzan remembered the idea that came to them. "Can we combine the energy of a 22-year-old with land to farm?"

The Sustainable Iowa Land Trust (SILT) was born from that notion. They used the rest of their life savings to buy 73 acres of farmland and set up a leasing program for farmers looking to plant regenerative organic farms. To raise additional funds, they pitched their project to Slow Money, a network of investors that sponsors small-scale sustainable farming ventures.

Suzan didn't stop there. She used her skills as an organizer to add acres to the trust. She pitched local landowners to see if they'd be willing to make their land available to future farmers through an easement or outright donation.

"We're not here to convince you, Joe Farmer, who's been doing this all your life, that you're doing it wrong. We're not here to judge you, and we're not here to tell you to change. We're here to say that if you want to leave a legacy for the future, we know there's a market. People have never stopped eating. And we know there are problems with our water, our air, and our climate, and no matter what you think is the cause, you've got to agree that there's nothing wrong with growing some food for your neighbors."

In making her case, Suzan, who's from New York state, had to adapt to the cultural differences in Midwestern communication. "One of my jobs as a New Yorker is, first of all, learn when to shut up and learn how to listen better, because there's more in the silences than anything else." Suzan was persistent and patient in working through the cultural divide. Her efforts paid off, and she ended up securing over 700 acres for the land trust.

She gave an example of what that means for farmers who apply for a lease with the land trust. "You get 40 acres of land plus a four-bedroom home, six out-buildings, and fencing for $12,000 a year to start." That yearly price goes up $1,000 a year for two years. After a three-year probationary period, "we'll offer you a 20-year lease on the land, and you can gain equity through the house and the barn. You can sell the house to the next farmer."

At the time of this writing, there were five farms on SILT land. That might not seem like much compared to the many 1,000-acre operations that surround them. Suzan estimated though that at full production their land could feed 110,000 Iowans with a diverse diet of fruits, veggies, grains, and meat. Ironically, though Iowa grows more crops than any state other than California, they import 88 percent of their own food. SILT's goal is not to feed the world, but to nourish their neighbors. "Monsanto's slogan is, 'We feed the world.' We just tell folks, 'That's okay. You feed the world, we'll feed Iowa.'"

SILT is one of many in a growing movement of land trusts that protect agricultural land and make it available to the next generation of farmers. Some are small and local, evolving from more general land trusts to include farming. Others are much larger. The Vermont Land Trust protects over half a million acres across the state.

In this mix is another type of organization. Groups of citizens in towns around the world are raising money to create their own farms. In France, the *Terre de Liens* movement has brought together 12,000 people to secure 200 farms in the French countryside. In Colorado, Poudre Valley Community Farms acquired 100 acres for a leasing program with local farmers. These properties go beyond growing food; they've created a cross between a sanctuary and a community estate. They provide a place for people to escape the stresses of the modern world and reconnect with the Earth. It's a place to heal the land as we heal ourselves.

Soul Fire Farm in Upstate New York is rooted in a dual healing of soil and self that spans generations. Co-founder Leah Penninam traces her journey into farming with her ancestors.

"There's a family story about our great-great-grandma, Susie Boyd, and many of the women in the community of the Dahomey region of West Africa. When everyone around them was being kidnapped and rounded up and they faced an uncertain future, they made a choice that astounds me even in this moment. They decided to take [seeds from] the okra, the millet, the black rice, and the cowpeas that their families had saved for generations, and to hide them in their braids. They didn't know where they were going, but they believed against all odds in a future on soil, and they believed in us that we would exist, and that they needed a legacy to pass on."

Nearly 200 years later, Leah is carrying on that legacy. She learned to farm in the countryside of central Massachusetts and the urban food gardens of Boston. While she eventually became a public-school teacher, she and her partner, Jonah Vitale-Wolff, still dreamed of having a farm of their own. For ten years, they saved everything they could. As a family of four with two kids, they squeezed into one bedroom of a shared house, didn't own a car, and lived on mostly rice and beans. Through frugality and determination, Leah managed to save $20,000 every year.

Their family eventually ended up in Albany, New York, in a neighborhood where the nearest grocery story was a two-mile walk away. "When our neighbors found out we knew how to farm, there was a clamor. 'You need to start a farm for the people. I'll join. I'll be a customer. I want to visit.' And so this vision was really a community vision."

After years of searching, they finally found affordable land on a nearby hillside, which had been eroded by logging. When Leah stuck her shovel in the ground, it only went in seven inches before hitting hard clay. By contrast, some Midwestern topsoil runs several feet deep. "The neighbors around us shook their heads, like 'You cannot grow vegetables on this land.'"

Leah and Jonah were not deterred. They knew how to build soil. Working on urban gardens, they'd learned how to use the dirt to protect plants from lead contamination. Leah also looked back to the agricultural traditions of her African heritage. They mounded the soil with organic matter to give it depth, adapting techniques used by the Ovambo farmers of Namibia. They built terraces to make the hillside suitable for growing, following a Kenyan practice that involves gathering soil from the bottom of the slope and "throwing it upward" to form a level plot for growing. They then blanketed their terraces in cover crops, which Leah described as "alchemists that are able to take air and turn it into soil." After four years of building, they were ready to start growing food.

Their Albany neighbors were some of the first 20 families to join their Community Supported Agriculture (CSA) food subscription service. Today, they feed 80 to 100 families (varies year-to-year) every week, many of whom wouldn't otherwise have access to fresh produce. All of their members are low income, BIPOC (Black, Indigenous, people of color), and living in areas classified as "food deserts." "One member told us that their family 'would be eating only boiled pasta if it were not for this veggie box.'" Throughout the growing season, Soul Fire Farm delivers fresh produce directly to the doors of their members. "They call it Netflix for vegetables." The CSA model also helps the farm secure a larger percentage of the proceeds and maintain a consistent customer base. "We want to be not just environmentally sustainable, but really a model of financial solvency."

Their farm goes far beyond providing healthy food. They've created a training ground for ending injustice in the food system. Every summer they offer multiple courses for BIPOC folks to learn how to grow food, and many graduates go on to start their own community gardens and farms. They also set up a partnership with the county courts to provide an alternative to jail time for youth in the area. Instead of entering the criminal-justice system, young people are able to complete a 50-hour farm training at Soul Fire Farm and other community organizations. The training program also includes classes on financial literacy and other skills to prepare students for a life outside of the criminal justice system. "It was imperative that we interrupt the school-to-prison pipeline that demonizes and criminalizes our youth."

While a Black-owned farm in rural America is rare today, it wasn't always this way. Leah pointed out that in 1920, Black people owned 16 million acres of land, or 14 percent of the farmland, which was a higher percentage than they made up in the population. Fifty years later, 90 percent of that had been lost, the result of intimidation by hate groups like the Ku Klux Klan, discrimination by the USDA, and partition sales, combined with the draw of factory jobs that led to the Great Migration of Black folks out of the rural South. Today, less than one-and-a-half percent of farmland is owned by Black farmers. Soul Fire Farm is providing the skills to begin reversing this trend. Leah said that many graduates of their farm immersion program "are going 'home' to the South to revive land that is still in their families. They are part of a returning generation of Black farmers."

At the same time, Leah acknowledged the need to heal from the ancestral trauma that endures from the legacy of slavery. "Many of our people have confused the oppression that took place on land with the land itself. And so there's a lot of ancestral, almost cellular trauma that's associated with wild spaces," she said. "We do not stoop, sweat, harvest, or even get dirty, because we imagine that would revert us to bondage."

Yet Leah also sees a rich history of farming from both Indigenous and African heritages. "It's not so much that we are stepping into this white good-food movement." She pointed out that over 100 years ago, George Washington Carver had developed practices to build soil that helped Black farmers in rural Georgia. He even called this system "regenerative agriculture." Fannie Lou Hamer innovated on cooperative businesses, and Black, civil-rights-era farmers established the model of community land trusts that's gaining momentum today. "This has always been our movement, and history has done its best job to alienate us from land and to tell us that we don't belong and that it's not our story, but it's always been our story."

The healing of soil and soul may not be completed in our generation. It took many lifetimes to create the problems of today, and it will take more than one to recover. "In these challenging times it's very easy to give up, to lose hope, to just put Netflix on and chill, right? And I have to be reminded that if they [our ancestors] didn't give up on us, then who are we, in much less dire circumstances, to give up on our descendants?"

Leah and the people within and beyond this book are laying a foundation for the next generation to build upon. Today, the number of farms that regenerate the Earth may be small, but they're emerging everywhere. No matter where we come from, we possess a unique and valuable connection to the land. We can use it to rejuvenate the soil and empower people in the places we love. From eroded hillsides to over-tilled prairies and rainforests burned to ashes, we can begin to restore nature's bounty—and ourselves with it.

## KEEP EXPLORING

- *How can I support organizations and land trusts that enable the next generation of farmers to heal the soil and food systems?*

- *How can I support people who have been dispossessed of their land to reclaim it?*

- *If my community created its own farm or estate, what would it look like and where would it be?*

# What's Next

---

"TO ACCOMPLISH GREAT THINGS WE
MUST NOT ONLY ACT, BUT ALSO DREAM;
NOT ONLY PLAN, BUT ALSO BELIEVE."

—ANATOLE FRANCE

# PLANET ON THE MIND

&#9644;

I N WRAPPING UP THE BOOK, WE WANT TO REVISIT ONE OF OUR MAIN themes—the importance of our attitudes, emotions, and deeply held beliefs in determining how we respond to the climate crisis. New technologies and logistics are essential for healing the planet, but how we think and feel on the inside ultimately determines what we will act on and implement. If a brilliant solution comes along, but we don't trust it or understand it, it probably won't gain much traction.

Inspired attitudes and beliefs can spur us to action. But if our beliefs are based on archaic traditions, incorrect information, or emotional coping mechanisms, they can be a hindrance. A simple fear of change is a good example. Overhauling energy, food, and manufacturing systems around the world can stoke resistance and make us want to cling to what's familiar. Images of an impending climate catastrophe can also paralyze and immobilize us. Even tiny doses of shame or guilt for not living a perfectly green lifestyle can make it tempting to just give up. This chapter is a deeper investigation into this cognitive side of our response to climate change.

But where did our beliefs about our relationship with nature come from? After all, the beliefs with the most power over us are those that we may be unaware of. Some of our beliefs are, of course, based on personal experience and how nature was presented to us by our parents and our peers. Those influences are unique to each of us. But it may be surprising to know how much our views about nature in the Western world have been hardwired into us.

The power of religion to influence mindsets in a society is massive. Christianity, Islam, and Judaism, the dominant religions of the West, share very similar approaches to interacting with nature. One approach is dominion, in which we control, dominate, and extract from nature. The other is stewardship, cultivation, and tending to the natural world. This is somewhat in contrast to the principal Eastern religions that depict a human being as a living, integrated *part of* nature rather than a separate agent that's acting *upon nature*.

Fast-forward to the 18th century in the West when nature and wilderness were wrapped in myth and legend and still widely seen as things to fear or conquer. Great beasts, tempestuous weather, vast deserts and oceans, and inconsistent harvests were our foes to vanquish and supersede. The European Enlightenment's empirical observation and the scientific method moved us away from fear and superstition and toward a rational and quantifiable assessment of the natural world. Two choices emerged: either sequester and protect nature (local and national parks), or exploit it for our needs (capitalism). Here we see the seeds of both the modern environmental movement and the opposing push to let free-market capitalism run free without limitation. This reflected and reinforced the two-fold approach to nature within Western religions that presents a simultaneous caring for and domination over the natural environment.

Then came the industrial revolution. Harvesting raw materials to feed voracious production lines became necessary to supply the world with a huge array of new products. Pumping coal into steel mills and felling forests to create furniture, ships, and houses was essential to keep the economy going. This fortified the idea that a thriving economy is at odds with a healthy natural world.

Conflicting ideas about how to treat nature have been downloaded into our individual and collective psyche by multiple institutions that form the "hard drive" of Western society. Every day, it is up to us to choose which relationship with nature—stewardship or domination—that we want our lifestyle, our community, our businesses, and our institutions to cultivate.

In this book, we propose moving beyond these contradictory approaches to nature by showing that the best solutions to the planet's problems are synergistic rather than zero-sum. Synergistic solutions generate positive effects that are interwoven across multiple sectors, while zero-sum tactics boost one area by depleting another. For example, regenerative farming sequesters carbon in the soil, increases production, and enhances human health. While conventional farming can increase harvests, it simultaneously pollutes water and soil, and over time harms animals and humans.

This same zero-sum logic feeds the common belief that protecting the environment is necessarily bad for business. Yet this is only true in the old model, where commerce is in disharmony with nature. "It's not an investment if it ruins the planet," renowned ecologist, Vandana Shiva said to the audience in a recent talk she gave in Berkeley. When economic productivity aligns with nature's cycles, rather than a "zero sum," what results is an "unlimited sum" in that the natural world, the economy, and human society are all enhanced simultaneously. What at first seems like a pipe dream is, in fact, the best way forward.

Another shift in mindset is to see this crisis as a huge opportunity for innovation and collaboration rather than just a time to suffer through and endure environmental degradation. In the spirit of Plato's "Necessity is the mother of invention," we can allow the stress of this crisis to spark a sense of urgency and a creative spirit rather than guilt and defeatism.

For so many of us, the scariest word associated with climate change is "sacrifice." Living more sustainably in order to mitigate climate change is strongly associated with making lifestyle sacrifices—like suffering in a cold house to save energy, riding crowded public transit, or giving up our favorite foods. According to Michael Maniates and John M. Meyer, the editors of *The Environmental Politics of Sacrifice*, we often relate being "eco-friendly" with giving up our luxuries, and that just doesn't sound very inviting.

But the reality is, living with cancerous air, polluted waterways, and vanishing ecosystems—those are true sacrifices. That's because living in *dis*harmony with nature, and the ensuing pollution and toxification of our environment, make our world a less healthy place.

Many psychologists argue that using the threat of climate change as a motivator for action fails to trigger our sympathetic nervous system—that is, our fight-or-flight response. We're wired through our evolution as a species to respond to abrupt, local changes, and we perceive climate change as part of a much slower and more distant threat than, say, a charging tiger. Haydn Washington and John Cook, the authors of *Climate Change Denial*, borrow from Freud when they suggest that not responding to, or even ignoring, climate change may be an act of psychological self-preservation because it's such an overwhelming truth to accept, and on a scale that feels unmanageable.

To understand what's going on in our heads as we confront one of the greatest threats to human existence, I sat down with Dr. Michael Ranney. He's a professor of psychology and education at UC Berkeley, just a quick bike ride from the college campus where I teach. Dr. Ranney researches some of the specific factors that make someone accept, deny, or simply ignore climate change. Even though by most accounts, climate change denial is steadily declining, the psychology behind it holds fascinating insights for other biases that we may harbor.

Sometimes the difference between denial and acceptance is simpler than we think. "When asked if climate change is real, we are more likely to say 'Yes' if it's hot outside that day," said professor Ranney. "In fact," he said, "if you are holding a hot beverage when someone is discussing climate change, you are more likely to accept global warming."

As we chatted at a local café on what happened to be a record-breaking day of heat, professor Ranney's data seemed more urgent than ever. He told me that "acceptance of climate change often comes down to money, especially if someone is personally affected fi nancially." He pointed to a phenomenon that's happening in Miami. "Due to sea-level rise, flood-prone property is noticeably dropping in value relative to less flood-prone and more inland property. This fact is likely more convincing to those denying climate change than other statistics that may not affect them as directly."

"Also, a simple lack of accurate scientific information is definitely a component in climate change denial," he said. "In our first study, we interviewed about 300 adults in the US and zero could explain the fundamental mechanism that is generating Earth's warming. Many researchers don't realize or accept this 'wisdom deficit' because they think that climate change denial is essentially based on politics or culture, but that turns out to be only partially true."

I asked Dr. Ranney for the biggest takeaway of his research. "We need to disseminate galvanizing scientific information on climate change to wake people up," he said. "If there's little motivation, people won't change. But if there is extreme motivation (such as apocalyptic predictions)—and if people don't realize how readily we can address the situation—then that can transform into a form of helplessness. At that point, people may just give up and say, 'We're screwed.'"

How we frame messages about crises directly impacts how people react to them. We've seen this played out in the widely varied narratives and responses to COVID-19 across the world. In response to a frightening, yet slow-moving disaster like climate change, it's even more difficult for us to mobilize without clear and compelling solutions. That's why throughout this book, we've focused on how the challenges of climate change consistently reveal opportunities to build something better. Outdated industrial and commercial systems that exploit nature can be replaced by systems of productivity and income that recognize, synergize with, and even mimic the natural world.

These changes should have been made decades or centuries ago, but conditions apparently weren't bad enough to move us towards collective action. The detriment, but also the blessing, of this acute crisis is that it's finally waking us up. We're now aware of how bad things have been for some time, and how much better they truly can be. While climate change developments are sobering and real, at the same time there's huge potential for positive change by an informed, galvanized globe.

In the realms of energy, food, industry, and cities specific mental shifts can help facilitate that change. A few generations ago in this country, households generally provided for their own energy and food. But now that's handled by "someone else," so it's easy to feel detached and uninvolved. Returning to an active decision-making role in how our energy and food are provided is essential. The same applies to industry. Apathetic consumers *accept* the quality of products that are offered, but informed citizens can *guide* the underlying system of consumption to a better state. In cities, our mental shift is one of scale. Urban areas got so big that we lost touch with the power of the small and the local. Neighborhood-level change and community-based organizations are perhaps the most powerful vehicle for grassroots change.

A crisis can feel overwhelming until we begin to see its massive opportunities for growth and its role in the bigger picture of our overall evolution. Ultimately, our mindsets need to evolve as much as our actions and institutions do. From there, we can kick-start a renaissance in the realms of energy, industry, cities, and farms. Those deep shifts make it possible to actually emerge from this crisis stronger than we were before.

# AN ERA OF COMMUNITY

---

WHERE DO *WE* AS INDIVIDUALS BEGIN IN THIS JOURNEY TO BUILD A better world? Should we go out and advocate for community-choice energy, or create a microgrid for the neighborhood? Should we get involved in developing ways to endlessly regenerate our natural resources? Should we transform an abandoned lot into a community development, or make main street more walkable? Should we start a neighborhood garden, or organize a community estate?

When these big questions overwhelmed me, I told Greg that I had to take a moment to think small. I looked for the beauty and strength already around me in my own backyard.

I figured one, relatively simple first step (pre-COVID-19) was to start with a neighborhood party. When the month of May rolled around, bringing warm weather and long afternoons, I threw a backyard party for my neighbors. I went door-to-door and invited everyone on the block. The get-together had no agenda. It was just a chance for everyone on our street to meet and mingle. I spent about $50 on supplies, and everyone else contributed to the potluck.

I'd been going about my own life, rushing from my car to my couch or from one destination to the next, never knowing the people around me. Now, I was in the same backyard with everyone on the block, enjoying a moment of late-spring sunshine with the former strangers next door. Kids ran around and played, while the adults sipped margaritas. My partner, Lila, and I invited our friends, too, including Greg and his family. People of different generations, interests, and backgrounds all mixed together. In the process, I learned that one neighbor hosts a radio show, one organizes disaster-prep workshops, and another is a metal worker. It was a chance to build new relationships, while learning about our collective skills as a block.

I also learned that there were already many friendships between neighbors, and an existing group of people hosted a block party every year. I looked at what other neighborhood organizations in the area were doing. Oakland has a long history of neighborhood associations, and many do great work in their communities. The Golden Gate Community Association and Longfellow Community Association were an inspiration as I thought about how to organize in my own neighborhood.

I decided to start small and began with a block club. I invited my neighbors to share their vision for our community. Only three people showed up at that first meeting. By the fourth monthly gathering, 11 people were there. After a series of brainstorming sessions, we decided on a few initiatives, naturally organizing around our personal interests.

The gardeners made plans to plant a corridor of flowers in our median strips to support bees and butterflies. My wife, Lila, started a relationship with an existing shelter on our block for women and children escaping domestic violence. Another neighbor and I coordinated parties and events. In the era of COVID-19, we stopped in-person parties and meetings, but our connections continued. One neighbor organized a so-cially distanced stoop gathering, parents formed an impromptu school-house and childcare group, Lila raised money for the women's shelter, and I started a weekly newsletter, for a time, on supporting local busi-nesses and causes.

Our tiny group of neighbors represented the potential of just one block. And there were 40 blocks in my neighborhood alone. I often dreamed about each one doing something for those in need, growing some food, or sharing their skills. I thought of all the bigger projects and parties that could happen if we expanded just one step further to the neighborhood level. Neighborhoods could then team up with other neighborhoods to share ideas, resources, and memories. I imagined one day being able to travel anywhere in the world and walk into a meeting where I can hear another vision for positive change, offer my perspective and support, and make new friends. Maybe then we could work toward bigger things like full-blown community farms or independent micro-grids.

Before COVID-19 hit, I'd decided to look beyond my own block to collaborate with others already working to empower local visions for the future. In determining what to do, I asked myself four questions:

1. What vision or project for a better world and planet compels me?

2. What's meaningful and impactful to the people around me?

3. Who's already working on that vision?

4. What can we offer each other?

After going to a handful of events, I found one organization that answered all those questions for me. The Community Democracy Project is an Oakland-based organization working to let residents choose how the city spends their tax money. We gathered signatures for an initiative that would create forums in each neighborhood where people could discuss their ideas for the city and vote on how they think its resources should be used. Though we were 2,000 signatures short of the 37,000 needed to make it on the ballot, going out and talking to thousands of people about their perspective on the city's future was an incredible growth experience. I stayed involved with the group to plan the next campaign because of the friends I made along the way. Eventually, Lila and I would move to a new town where we hope to support local leaders and give back to the community there.

It's easy to assume that the quickest way to create widespread change is to take it to the highest level of government and scale it top-down. But think of how quickly change can happen when a call to action ripples through a million organized communities. We as a society can create change at a viral pace. And we can do it in a way that best reflects the needs and character of each place, drawing upon *us* as the resident experts.

It's also here, at the local level, that we're able to connect with something simple and eternal. Since the beginning of our time on Earth, we've come together to share food, stories, and visions around a fire. A street in West Texas and a village in West Africa might not have much in common, but both enjoy the act of breaking bread. The great project of the future is not just to create global agreements, but to bring us together through simple yet meaningful personal interactions. The goal is to share our sense of community with other communities, to laugh together, and to learn from each other.

We, the authors of this book, believe that a bright green future will not be won solely in political battles or global struggles, but also in backyard parties and community meetings. We've seen dramatic revolutions where people march through the streets. It's now time for an ordinary revolution where billions of us gather for an afternoon with friends to sketch out the neighborhood, community, or city of our dreams. It may not be as glamorous, but ultimately, it's more meaningful in our everyday lives. There will still be great leaders, but they will live down the block.

It's a return to the wisdom of nature that's been here all along. An ecosystem doesn't find its strength in dominant species, but in the interdependence of many coexisting in an eternal balance. As the everyday heroes in this book show us, it's our communities that will ultimately save the planet and forge a better future for humanity. The great superpowers of Earth will rise and fall with time. Great communities will flourish forever.

# Acknowledgements

W HEN WE THINK OF ACKNOWLEDGEMENTS WE IMAGINE A PARTY. Everyone who made this book possible is gathered together in a sunny meadow or great hall. This book is the celebration of many stories from many places. And though the characters have only met in the world of ink and paper, maybe one day we'll convene for real.

In addition to those who fill the pages of this book, we'd like to thank those between the lines. Expertise from these folks steered the book in many ways. Thank you to Adrian White and William Lorentzen, Alexandra McGee, Andres Alayza, Andrew Krowne, Ann Adams, Ann Starodaj, Bamm Brewer, Barry Watkins, Bill and Chloe Parker, Brian Haynes, Cara Carmichael, Chris Stern, Christine Moseley, Clinton Wilson, Cynthia Powers, Dan Solomon, Elisabeth Winkler, Evelyn Butler, Fred Iutzi, Frederick Bjørndal, Gary Gero, Gert van Exel, Gus Yellowhair, Jason Kibbey, Jenine Windeshausen, Jenn Jenkins, Jennifer Bryan, Jennifer Gerholdt, Jennifer Holmgren, Jennifer Nini, Jeri Baker, Joe Emerson, Joel Levin, Jon Ramsay, Joseph Kunkel, Justin Hegarty, Keefe Keeley, Lauren Hiene, Lindsey Lusher Shute, Mary Johnson, Matt Jungclaus, Melvin Johnson, Mike Gold, Nancy Ranney, Nick DeCristofaro, Nicolas Buttin, Nicole Miller, Norman Garrick, Olivia Muiru, Pamela Leonard, Paul Gambill, Paul Mackie, Peter Donnovan, Peter Norton, Rachel McManus, Robbie Orvis, Roger Leakey, Ron Rebenitsch, Sallie Calhoun, Tom Figel, Tom Lamar, Victor Olgyay, and Wes Reeves.

We'd like to give a big thanks to our editor, Mary Kole whose skillful touch transformed 200-plus pages of rough prose into something pass-able for popular non-fiction. Giant thanks are also due to the illustrator, Oručević Emir of Pulp Studios who went through over 90 variations on the cover to arrive back at a small tweak to one of his first designs.

Thank you to our friends and family who took the time to read early drafts of the book and provide feedback: Atul Singh, Brian Fliesher, Bri-an Velasquez, Cole Short, Dana L. Davis, Emily Shapiro, Faye Schwartz, Jay Cohen, Jean Cohen, Jondy Cohen, Keegan Cohen, Laura Cox, Lila Frisher, Paul Durrenburger, Rin Johnson, Stephanie Schwartz, Zeph Co-lombatto, and Zoë Emmanuel. Of particular note, Greg would like to acknowledge his academic mentors, Yi-Fu Tuan, Greg Knapp, and Karl Butzer.

Last, but not least, thank you to our loved ones who supported us through the challenges of writing a book, Chanel Haynes-Schwartz, Faye Schwartz, and Lila Frisher.

No book was ever written in a vacuum. Every sentence was penned by a thousand hands of influence, both visible and invisible. Thank you to the teachers, students, mentors, family, friends, writers, characters, strangers, and spirits who've shaped our hearts and minds.

# BIBLIOGRAPHY

### Doorway to a Bright Green Future

"Building Resilient Communities: A Moral Responsibility | Nick Tilsen | TEDxRapidCity." Performance by Nick Tilsen, *YouTube*, TEDx, 14 Jul. 2015, www.youtube.com/watch?v=e2Re-KrQNa4, accessed June 2018.

### Human—Nature

Butzer, Karl W. "Cultural Ecology" In *Geography in America*, edited by Gary L. Gaile, 192-208. Merrill Publishing Company, 1989.

Rogers, Heather. *Green Gone Wrong: How Our Economy Is Undermining the Environmental Revolution*. Scribner, 2010.

### Energy

Konisky, Ansolabehere. *Cheap and Clean: How Americans Think about Energy in the Age of Global Warming*. The MIT Press, 2014.

Glover PC, Economides MJ, *Energy and Climate Wars: How Naive Politicians, Green Ideologues, and Media Elites Are Undermining the Truth about Energy and Climate*. Continuum; 2010.

Lacey, Stephen, host. "What if Utilities are to Blame for Wildfires." *The Energy Gang*, 21 Nov. 2018.

Botkin DB. *Powering the Future: A Scientist's Guide to Energy Independence*. 1 edition. Upper Saddle River, N.J: FT Press; 2010.

Klare M. *Rising Powers, Shrinking Planet: The New Geopolitics of Energy by Michael Klare*. Metropolitan Books; 2008.

Diesendorf, Mark. *Sustainable Energy Solutions for Climate Change*. Routledge; 2014.

Brown LR, Adams E, Larsen J, Roney JM. *The Great Transition: Shifting from Fossil Fuels to Solar and Wind Energy*. 1 edition. New York: W. W. Norton & Company; 2015.

## Symbiotic Grid

Bakke, Gretchen. *The Grid: The fraying wires between Americans and our energy future*. Bloomsbury, 2017.

Hodges, Jeremy. "Green Energy Producers Just Installed Their First Trillion Watts." *Bloomberg New Energy Finance*, 1 Aug. 2018, https://www.bloomberg.com/news/articles/2018-08-02/green-energy-capacity-passes-a-trillion-watts.

Poindexter, Nicole. Phone interview. 17 May 2017.

McKibben, Bill. "The Race to Solar-Power Africa." The New Yorker, The New Yorker, 26 Jun. 2017, www.newyorker.com/magazine/2017/06/26/the-race-to-solar-power-africa.

Clendaniel, Morgan. "The Developing World Can Leapfrog Dirty Coal And Go Straight To Clean Energy." *Fast Company*, 5 Feb. 2016, www.fastcompany.com/3056313/the-developing-world-can-leapfrog-dirty-coal-and-go-straight-to-clean-energy.

Loutan, Clyde. Phone interview. 4 Jul. 2017.

Loutan, Clyde, and Vahan Gevorgian. "Using Renewables to Operate a Low Carbon Grid." *California ISO*, 18 Jan. 2017, http://www.caiso.com/Documents/UsingRenewablesToOperateLow-CarbonGrid.pdf.

Dyson, Mandel, Bronski, Lehrman, Morris. *The Economics of Demand Flexibility: How "Flexiwatts" Create Quantifiable Value for Customers and the Grid*. Rocky Mountain Institute, 2015.

Penn, Ivan "California invested heavily in solar power. Now there's so much that other states are sometimes paid to take it." *LA Times*, 22 Jun. 2017. https://www.latimes.com/projects/la-fi-electricity-solar/

## Power to Grow Wealth for All

"Wind Energy in the United States." American Wind Energy Association, 2019, https://www.awea.org/wind-101/basics-of-wind-energy/wind-facts-at-a-glance

Shersen, Steve. Phone interview. 26 Feb. 2018.

Shersen, Nick. Phone interview. 27 Feb. 2018.

Rebenitsch, Ron. Phone interview. 27 Feb. 2018.

Williams, Darin. Personal interview. 20 Mar. 2018.

Little, Amanda. *Power Trip: The Story of America's Love Affair with Energy.* Harper Collins, 2010.

Brown, Lester. *The Great Transition: Shifting from Fossil Fuels to Solar and Wind Energy.* W.W. Norton, 2015.

Thompson, Stephen A. "Crow Lake Wind Powers Up: Nation's Largest Co-Op Wind Farm Includes Community- and College-Owned Turbines." *Rural Cooperatives. U.S. Department of Agriculture, Rural Business - Cooperative Service*, Mar.-Apr. 2011, https://www.questia.com/magazine/1G1-253536380/crow-lake-wind-powers-up-nation-s-largest-co-op-wind

Weisz, Dawn. Phone interview. 5 Jun. 2019.

McGee, Alexandra. Personal interview. 9 May 2018.

"MCE 2019 Integrated Resource Plan: Exceeding State Targets." Accelerating California's Clean Energy Future. Marin Clean Energy, 2019, https://www.mcecleanenergy. org/wp-content/uploads/2018/12/2019-IRP-highlights-flyer_12102018.pdf.

Lucero, Fred. 16 May 2018. Personal interview.

Brito, Jonathan. 18 May 2018. Personal interview.

Leonard, Pamela. Phone interview. 16 May 2018.

Windeshausen, Jenine. Phone interview. 29 Jun. 2018.

Gero, Gary. Phone interview. 16 May 2018.

Tovar, Jessica. Personal interview. 18 May 2018.

Henderson, Annie. Phone interview. 15 May 2018.

Fairchild, Denise, and Al Weinrub. *Energy Democracy: Advancing Equity in Clean Energy Solutions.* Island Press, 2017.

**The Future is Electric**

Popple, Ryan. Phone interview. 29 Jun. 2018.

Shindell, Drew T. "The Social Cost of Atmospheric Release." *Climatic Change*, vol. 130, no. 2, 2015, pp. 313–326., doi:10.1007/s10584-015-1343-0.

"Driving Harm: Health and Community Impacts of Living near Truck Corridors." *Trade, Health and Environment Impact Report*, Jan. 2012, https://envhealthcenters. usc.edu/wp-content/uploads/2016/11/Driving-Harm.pdf.

Cavallo, Michele. "Oil Prices and Inflation." *Federal Reserve Bank of San Francisco*, 3 Oct. 2008, www.frbsf.org/economic-research/publications/economic-letter/2008/october/ oil-prices-inflation/.

Stringer, David, and Jie Ma. "Where 3 Million Electric Vehicle Batteries Will Go When They Retire." *Bloomberg*, 27 Jun. 2018. www.bloomberg.com/news/features/2018-06-27/where-3-million-electric-vehicle-batteries-will-go-when-they-retire.

Guille, Christophe, and George Gross. "A Conceptual Framework for the Vehicle-to-Grid (V2G) Implementation." *Energy Policy*, vol. 37, no. 11, 2009, pp. 4379–4390., doi:10.1016/j.enpol.2009.05.053.

Voelcker, John. "Tesla Model S Battery Life: What the Data Show so Far." *Green Car Reports*, 27 Apr. 2017, www.greencarreports.com/news/1110149_tesla-model-s-battery-life-what-the-data-show-so-far.

"Moixa and National Grid in Consortium to Study How to Reward Drivers Who Use Electric Car Batteries to Support Power Network." *Moixa*, 27 Feb. 2018, www.moixa.com/press-release/moixa-national-grid-consortium-study-reward-drivers-use-electric-car-batteries-support-power-network/.

Hamelink, Marten. Phone interview. 18 May 2018.

McMahon, Jeff. "Electric Vehicles Cost Less Than Half As Much To Drive." *Forbes Magazine*, 16 Jan. 2018, www.forbes.com/sites/jeffmcmahon/2018/01/14/electric-vehicles-cost-less-than-half-as-much-to-drive/.

Hall, Dale, and Nic Lutsey. "Emerging Best Practices for Electric Vehicle Charging Infrastructure." *The International Council on Clean Transportation*, Oct. 2017, https://www.theicct.org/sites/default/files/publications/EV-charging-best-practices_ICCT-white-paper_04102017_vF.pdf.

## Gardens in the Coalfields

Wrenn, Marilyn. Phone interview. 18 Mar. 2019.

"West Virginia Opioid Summary." *National Institute on Drug Abuse*, Mar. 2019, www.drugabuse.gov/opioid-summaries-by-state/west-virginia-opioid-summary.

"Reclaim Appalachia - Seppi Demo." Vimeo, *JJN Multimedia*, Jun. 2018, vimeo.com/245456581.

"Converting Mining-Impacted Lands." *Reclaim Appalachia*, reclaimappalachia.com/about-us/.

Casto, James. "Coalfield Development Corp. Working to End Coal Country's Cycle of Poverty." *WV News*, 15 Jan. 2018, www.wvnews.com/news/wvnews/coalfield-development-corp-working-to-end-coal-country-s-cycle/article_914c5a41-6991-50de-b5ad-42848e39aa60.html.

Dennison, Brandon, performer. Rebuilding Coal Country- Coalfield Development +

Stand Together. YouTube, *Stand Together Foundation*, 19 Sept. 2018, www.youtube. com/watch?v=6TDUY_IdhrY&t=1s.

## Industry

Forbes, Megan, host. "Garbage Patches: How Gyres Take Our Trash Out to Sea." NOAA Ocean Podcast: Episode 14, *National Oceanic and Atmospheric Administration*, 18 Mar. 2018. oceanservice.noaa.gov/podcast/mar18/nop14-ocean-garbage-patches.html.

Gudynas, Eduardo. "Buen Vivir: today's tomorrow." *Development* 54.4: 441-447. 2011.

Jason, Bittel. "A Single Discarded Fishing Net Can Keep Killing for Centuries." *NRDC*, 17 May 2018, www.nrdc.org/onearth/single-discarded-fishing-net-can-keep-killing-centuries.

Humes, Edward. *Garbology: Our Dirty Love Affair With Trash*. Penguin Books, 2012.

LeBlanc, Rick. "Textile and Garment Recycling Facts and Figures." *The Balance Small Business*, 27 Apr. 2019, www.thebalancesmb.com/textile-recycling-facts-and-figures-2878122.

## Industry as an Ecosystem

Holmes, D.E., and J.A. Smith. "Biologically Produced Methane as a Renewable Energy Source." *Advances in Applied Microbiology*, 2016, pp. 1–61., doi:10.1016/bs.aambs.2016.09.001.

Leopold, Aldo. "The Land Ethic." In *A Sand County Almanac: And Sketches Here and There*, 201-226. Oxford University Press, 1949.

Schauer-Gimenez, Anne. Phone interview. 20 Apr. 2017.

Schauer-Gimenez, Anne. Personal interview. 12 Jun. 2017.

Setala, Outi. "Microplastic Contamination in Aquatic Environments: an Emerging Matter of Environmental Urgency." *Elsevier*, 2018, pp. 339–363.

McDonough, William, and Michael Braungart. *Cradle to Cradle*. North Point Press, 2007.

Holgate, Peter. Phone interview. 4 May 2017.

Klein, Peter. *Ghana: Digital Dumping Ground*. Public Broadcasting Service, 23 Jun. 2009, www.pbs.org/frontlineworld/stories/ghana804/.

Schaller, R.R. "Moore's Law: Past, Present and Future." *IEEE Spectrum*, Jun. 1997, ieeexplore.ieee.org/document/591665/.

Minter, Adam. "The Burning Truth Behind an E-Waste Dump in Africa." *Smithsonian*

*Institution*, 13 Jan. 2016, www.smithsonianmag.com/science-nature/burning-truth-behind-e-waste-dump-africa-180957597/.

Pearce, Fred. *Confessions of an Eco-Sinner: Tracking down the Sources of My Stuff.* Boston: Beacon Press, 2009.

Nkulu, Célestin Banza Lubaba, et al. "Sustainability of Artisanal Mining of Cobalt in DR Congo." *Nature*, 14 Sept. 2018, www.nature.com/articles/s41893-018-0139-4.

Baker, Steve. Phone interview. 4 Feb 2019.

Kilkelley, James. Phone interview. 5 Apr. 2017.


## Infinite Wardrobe

"World of Change: Shrinking Aral Sea." *NASA Earth Observatory*, 2018, earthobservatory.nasa.gov/world-of-change/aral_sea.php.

Flynn, Stacy. Phone interview. Apr. 12 2017.

Flynn, Stacy. Phone interview. Jan. 9, 2019.

Daniels, Jess. Phone interview. Mar. 13 2019.

Dirksen, Kirsten, director. "150 Mile Wardrobe: Local Fiber, Real Color, P2P Economy." Performance by Rebecca Burgess, YouTube, Kirsten Dirksen, 20 Sept. 2011, www.youtube.com/watch?v=rEJmXmTFpMg.


## Immortal Forest

Constantz, Brent. Phone interview. 22 May 2018.

"Stanford Seminar: Carbon Sequestration." Performance by Brent Constantz, YouTube, *Stanford University*, 5 Jan. 2017, www.youtube.com/watch?v=XvtHPF1ng0s.

Wise, Alex, host. "Brent Constantz: Concrete Plans." *SeaChange Radio*, 10 Jul. 2018.

Pooler, Michael. "Cleaning up Steel Is Key to Tackling Climate Change." *Financial Times*, 1 Jan. 2019, www.ft.com/content/3bcbcb60-037f-11e9-99df-6183d3002ee1.

Hughes, J. Donald. "Ancient Deforestation Revisited." *Journal of the History of Biology*, vol. 44, no. 1, 2010, pp. 43–57., doi:10.1007/s10739-010-9247-3.

Denevan, William. "The Pristine Myth: The Landscape of the Americas in 1492," *Annals of the Association of American Geographers*, 82(3), 1992.

Van Lugt, Pablo. Phone interview. 24 Apr. 2017.

Sonter, Laura J., et al. "Mining Drives Extensive Deforestation in the Brazilian Amazon." *Nature Communications*, vol. 8, no. 1, 2017, doi:10.1038/s41467-017-00557-w.

## People, Planet, Prosperity

Harvey, David. "Population, Resources and the Ideology of Science." *Economic Geography* 50:256-57, 1974.

Schwartz GJ. *The role of women in payment for environmental services programs in Osa, Costa Rica.* Gender, Place & Culture. 2017;24(6):890-910. doi:10.1080/096636 9X.2017.1342603

Senard, Mathieu. Personal interview. 23 Apr. 2018.

Orvis, Robbie. Phone interview. 23 Jul. 2018.

Robinson, Rod. Phone interview. 28 May 2018.

Daugergne, Peter, and Lister, Jane. *Eco-Business: A Big-Brand Takeover of Sustainability.* MIT Press, 2013.

Lowery, Brennan interview. 13 Oct 2018.

Howarth, Daren. Skype interview 23 Jun. 2018.


## Cities

Shoup, Donald. *The High Cost of Free Parking.* Taylor and Francis, New York: 2011.

Mumford, Lewis. *The Highway and the City.* Harcourt Brace, 1963.

Kostof, Spiro, and Richard Tobias. *The City Shaped: Urban Patterns and Meanings through History.* Bulfinch Press, 2012.

Vance, James. *The Continuing City: Urban Morphology in Western Civilization.* Johns Hopkins University Press, 1990.

Tuan, Yi-Fu. *Space and place: The perspective of experience.* U of Minnesota Press, 1977.

Tumber C. *Small, Gritty, and Green: The Promise of America's Smaller Industrial Cities in a Low-Carbon World.* Reprint edition. Cambridge, Massachusetts: The MIT Press; 2013.


## Ponzi Scheme

"Joe Minicozzi: The Cash Flow of Urbanism." Performance by Joe Minicozzi, YouTube, *Congress for the New Urbanism,* 9 Aug. 2016, www.youtube.com/watch?v=p-FC_Q4WQKVk.

Bellis, Rayla, et al. "Repair Priorities 2014." Smart Growth America, Taxpayers for Common Sense, 2014, www.smartgrowthamerica.org/app/legacy/documents/repair-priorities-2014.pdf.

Frank, Thomas. "Civil Engineers Say Fixing Infrastructure Will Take $4.6 Trillion." *CNN Money*, 9 Mar. 2017, money.cnn.com/2017/03/09/news/infrastructure-report-card/index.html.

"What Is a STROAD?" Performance by Strong Towns, YouTube, *Strong Towns*, 1 Mar. 2018, www.youtube.com/watch?v=OZ1HhLq-Huo.

Marohn, Charles. "How to Turn a Stroad into a Street (or a Road)." *Strong Towns*, 15 Feb. 2018, www.strongtowns.org/journal/2018/2/15/how-to-turn-a-stroad-into-a-street-or-a-road.

Marohn, Charles. "Slow the Cars." Strong Towns, 16 Jan. 2018, www.strongtowns.org/journal/2018/1/15/slow-the-cars.

Suh, Rhea. "We Can't Assume Our Water Is Safe to Drink. But We Can Fix It." *National Geographic*, Mar. 2019, www.nationalgeographic.com/magazine/2019/03/drinking-water-safety-in-united-sates-can-be-fixed/.

## Guerilla Tactics and the Master Plan

"A Better Block | Jason Roberts | TEDxUTA." Performance by Jason Roberts, YouTube, *TEDx*, 29 Jun. 2016, www.youtube.com/watch?v=8HTkBTnZ9D4.

Sadik-Khan, Janette, and Seth Solomonow. *Streetfight: Handbook for an Urban Revolution*. Penguin Books, 2017.

Stempak, Nicole. "How Music Has Helped One Neighborhood Connect with Its Past and Plan for Its Future." *Strong Towns*, 18 Jun. 2018, www.strongtowns.org/journal/2018/6/18/music-future-past-akron-kenmore.

Eller, Donnelle. "Rural Iowa Retail Woes: Malls Struggle as New Wave of Store Closures Hits Small Towns." *Des Moines Register*, 4 Jun. 2018, www.desmoinesregister.com/story/money/business/2018/05/31/rural-iowa-retail-shopping-younkers-herberger-kmart-sears-jcpenny-mall-closing-stores-target-ottumwa/624676002/.

Lydon, Mike. "How One Weekend in Dallas Sparked a Movement for Urban Change." *Next City*, 20 Apr. 2015, nextcity.org/features/view/how-one-weekend-in-dallas-sparked-a-movement-for-urban-change.

Wassmer, Robert W. "Causes of Urban Sprawl in the United States: Auto Reliance as Compared to Natural Evolution, Flight from Blight, and Local Revenue Reliance." *Journal of Policy Analysis and Management*, vol. 27, no. 3, 2008, pp. 536–555., doi:10.1002/pam.20355.

Marohn, Charles, host. "Suburban Poverty Meets Sprawl Retrofit." *Strong Towns Podcast*, 24 Jun. 2018. https://www.strongtowns.org/journal/2018/7/12/suburban-poverty-meets-sprawl-retrofit.

Myers, David. "Belmar: 'Urbanizing' a Suburban Colorado Mall." *Urban Land Magazine*, 2013, urbanland.uli.org/development-business/belmar-urbanizing-a-suburban-colorado-mall/.

Buntin, Simmons B. "Agritopia in Gilbert, Arizona : UnSprawl Case Study." *Terrain.org*, 2009, www.terrain.org/unsprawl/24/.

Velten, Elspeth. "Enter an Arizona Design Utopia Redefining Urban Planning." *Architectural Digest*, 6 Aug. 2016, www.architecturaldigest.com/story/agritopia-arizona.

**Growing Economy Around Community**

"R. John Anderson: Code Hacking." Performance by John Anderson, Vimeo, *Incremental Development Alliance*, 2017, vimeo.com/204082235.

"Monte Anderson: Cultivating Neighborhoods." Performance by Monte Anderson, Vimeo, *Incremental Development Alliance*, 2017, vimeo.com/204035720.

Marohn, Charles, and Monte Anderson. "The Developer Who Was Desperate to Save a Struggling Neighborhood." *Strong Towns*, 24 Feb. 2016, www.strongtowns.org/journal/2016/2/23/the-developer-who-was-desperate-to-save-a-struggling-neighborhood.

Marohn, Charles, host. "Why is it so hard to get things built?" Strong Towns Podcast, *Strong Towns*, 7 Jun. 2018. https://www.strongtowns.org/journal/2018/6/6/why-is-it-so-hard-to-get-things-built.

Marohn, Charles, host. "How Parking Minimums Hinder Small-Scale Developers?" Strong Towns Podcast, *Strong Towns*, 21 Nov. 2017. https://www.strongtowns.org/journal/2017/11/21/how-parking-minimums-hinder-small-scale-developers

Sheir, Rebecca, host. "Self-Gentrifying in the Bronx." Placemakers, *Slate Magazine*, 21 August, 2016.

Ball, Lee, and Majora Carter. "Find Your Sustain Ability: Majora Carter "The Prophet of Local." Appalachian Magazine, *Appalachian State University*, 26 Jul. 2017.

"Hyde Lecture - Majora Carter." Performance by Majora Carter, YouTube, *University of Nebraska-Lincoln*, 27 Aug. 2018, www.youtube.com/watch?v=rzsQ2SBqu-8.

"Bronx Innovation Factory." The Bronx Cooperative Development Initiative, bcdi.nyc/bxif/.

Semuels, Alana. "How to Make Housing Affordable, Forever." *The Atlantic*, 6 Jul. 2015, www.theatlantic.com/business/archive/2015/07/affordable-housing-always/397637/.

"Majora Carter: Communities as Corporations." Performance by Majora Carter, YouTube, *Congress for the New Urbanism*, 10 Jul. 2017, www.youtube.com/watch?v=ACPV6B7zVwU.

Meyerson, Harold. "How the Bronx Came Back (But Didn't Bring Everyone Along)." *The American Prospect*, 15 Oct. 2015, prospect.org/article/how-bronx-came-back-didnt-bring-everyone-along.

## Thunder Valley

Iron Shell, Andrew. Personal interview. 23 Mar. 2018.

"Announcing Our New Executive Director: Tatewin Means." Performance by Nick Tilsen, and Tatewin Means, Vimeo, *Thunder Valley CDC*, 2018, vimeo.com/276387844.

Stephens, Bradley. "Nick Tilsen: Reimagining Comprehensive Community Change." Big Ideas for Better Places, performance by Nick Tilsen, episode 50, *CityWorks Xpo*, 8 May 2018.

"Building Resilient Communities: A Moral Responsibility | Nick Tilsen | TEDxRapidCity." Performance by Nick Tilsen, YouTube, *TEDx*, 14 Jul. 2015, www.youtube.com/watch?v=e2Re-KrQNa4.

Stasiowski, Jim. "Pine Ridge Speakers: History and Stereotypes Block Understanding between the Races." *Rapid City Journal Media Group*, 24 Oct. 2015, rapidcityjournal.com/news/local/pine-ridge-speakers-history-and-stereotypes-block-understanding-between-the/article_c5525de7-6f42-567f-8f8d-2c066b44c4ca.html.

Manning, Sarah S. "NDN Collective Founder Nick Tilsen Talks Building Indigenous Power." While Indigenous, performance by Nick Tilsen, episode 1, *NDN Collective*, 30 Sept. 2018.

## Farms

Bonanno A, Busch L, Friedland W, Gouveia L, Mingione E. *From Columbus to ConAgra: The Globalization of Agriculture and Food*. University Press of Kansas, 1994.

Boserup, Ester. *The Conditions of Agricultural Growth: The Economics of Agrarian Change under Population Pressure*. Allen and Unwin, 1965.

Goodland R, Anhang J. "Livestock and climate change: what if the key actors in climate change are... cows, pigs, and chickens?" *Worldwatch Institute*, 2009.

Cleveland DA. *Balancing on a Planet: The Future of Food and Agriculture*. First edition. Berkeley and Los Angeles, California: University of California Press; 2013.

Eshel G, Shepon A, Makov T, Milo R. "Land, irrigation water, greenhouse gas, and reactive nitrogen burdens of meat, eggs, and dairy production in the United States." *PNAS*. 2014;111(33):11996-12001. doi:10.1073/pnas.1402183111

Netting, Robert McC. *Smallholders, Householders: Farm Families and the Ecology of Inten-*

*sive, Sustainable Agriculture.* Stanford University Press, 1993.

Popkin BM. "The Nutrition Transition in the Developing World." *Development Policy Review.* 2003;21(5-6):581-597. doi:10.1111/j.1467-8659.2003.00225.x

## Soil Evaporates, Soil Grows

Blaikie P. and Brookfield H. *Land Degradation and Society.* CABDirect2, 1987.

Ohlson, Kristin. *The Soil Will Save Us: How Scientists, Farmers, and Foodies Are Healing the Soil to Save the Planet.* Rodale, 2014.

Schwartz, Judith D. *Cows Save the Planet and Other Improbable Ways of Restoring Soil to Heal the Earth.* Chelsea Green Publ., 2013.

Montgomery, David R. *Dirt: the Erosion of Civilizations.* University of California Press, 2008.

"Gulf of Mexico 'Dead Zone' Is the Largest Ever Measured." *National Oceanic and Atmospheric Administration,* 22 Aug. 2017, www.noaa.gov/media-release/gulf-of-mexico-dead-zone-is-largest-ever-measured.

Shepard, Mark. *Restoration Agriculture: Real-World Permaculture for Farmers.* Acres U.S.A., 2013.

Ajmone-Marsan, Paolo, et al. "On the Origin of Cattle: How Aurochs Became Cattle and Colonized the World." *Evolutionary Anthropology: Issues, News, and Reviews,* vol. 19, no. 4, 2010, pp. 148–157., doi:10.1002/evan.20267.

Wilson, Mike. "Profit Projection: In 2018, Grain Farms Will Barely Break Even." *Farm Progress,* 29 Aug. 2018, www.farmprogress.com/business/profit-projection-2018-grain-farms-will-barely-break-even.

Lal, Rattan. Phone interview. 5 Oct. 2017.

Fuller, Gail. Personal interview. 20 Mar. 2018.

Pedro, Guilherme De Andrade Vasconcelos, et al. "Determinants of the Brazilian Amazon Deforestation." *African Journal of Agricultural Research,* vol. 12, no. 3, 2017, pp. 169–176., doi:10.5897/ajar2016.11966.

Turrentine, Jeff. "How Did Farmer Brown Bring His Dying Land Back From the Brink?" *NRDC,* 28 Sept. 2018, www.nrdc.org/onearth/how-did-farmer-brown-bring-his-dying-land-back-brink.

## Stewards of the Prairie

Williams, Darin. Phone interview. 2 Mar. 2018.

Williams, Darin. Personal interview. 20 Mar. 2018.

"Bison Bellows: A Healthy Prairie Relies on Bison Poop (U.S. National Park Service)." National Parks Service, *U.S. Department of the Interior*, www.nps.gov/articles/bison-bellows-10-6-16.htm.

Klemm, Ken. (2018, March 18). Phone interview.

Klemm, Ken. Phone interview. 18 Mar. 2018.

Klemm, Ken. Personal interview. 19 Mar. 2018.

Klemm, Ken. Personal interview. 21 Mar. 2018.

## Wisdom of the Forest

Haslett-Marroquin, Reginaldo, and Per Andreassen. *In the Shadow of Green Man: My Journey from Poverty and Hunger to Food Security and Hope.* Acres U.S.A., 2017.

Haslett-Marroquin, Reginaldo. Phone interview. 12 Oct. 2018.

"Reginaldo Haslett Marroquin- Regenerate 2018." Performance by Reginaldo Haslett-Marroquin, YouTube, *Quivira Coalition*, 6 Dec. 2018, www.youtube.com/watch?v=QRftahifp38.

"Poultry-Centered Regenerative Agriculture." *Main Street Project*, mainstreetproject.org/.

Boa, Kofi. "Kofi Boa." *Green America*, www.greenamerica.org/personal-story/international-insights-kofi-boa-sows-seeds-soil-regeneration-ghana.

"Kofi Boa." Performance by Kofi Boa, YouTube, *No-Till on the Plains*, 26 Feb. 2016, www.youtube.com/watch?v=1F6lkLee5x8.

"Access To Education - Felicia Yeboah." *Centre for No-Till Agriculture*, centrefornotill.org/access-to-education.

Kleinman, P.J.A. "The Ecological Sustainability of Slash-and-Burn Agriculture." Agriculture, Ecosystems & Environment, vol. 52, no. 2-3, 1995, pp. 235–249., doi:10.1016/0167-8809(94)00531-i.

Lowder, Sarah K., et al. "The Number, Size, and Distribution of Farms, Smallholder Farms, and Family Farms Worldwide." *World Development*, vol. 87, 2016, pp. 16–29., doi:10.1016/j.worlddev.2015.10.041.

## Farm in the City

Grant, Beverly. Phone interview. 4 Mar. 2018.

Zandi, Haleh. Phone interview. 11 Mar. 2018

Crouch, Patrick. Phone interview. 16 Feb. 2018.

Davidson, Kate. "Detroit Has Tons of Vacant Land. But Forty Square Miles?" *Michigan Radio*, 18 Apr. 2012, www.michiganradio.org/post/detroit-has-tons-vacant-land-forty-square-miles.

Carmody, Dan. "A Growing City: Detroit's Rich Tradition of Urban Gardens Plays an Important Role in the City's Resurgence." *Urban Land Magazine*, 19 Mar. 2018, urbanland.uli.org/industry-sectors/public-spaces/growing-city-detroits-rich-tradition-urban-gardens-plays-important-role-citys-resurgence/.

Santo, Rachel, et al. *A Review of the Benefits and Limitations of Urban Agriculture.* John Hopkins, 2014, pp. 1–33, A Review of the Benefits and Limitations of Urban Agriculture.

**Back to the Land**

Erem, Suzan. Personal interview. 21 Mar. 2018.

Ramsay, Jon. "The Farmland Access Program Connects Farmers with Affordable Farmland." *Vermont Land Trust*, www.vlt.org/affordable-farmland.

Jon, Ramsay. Phone interview. 1 May 2018.

Jon, Ramsay. Phone interview. 3 May 2018.

Penniman, Leah, and Karen Washington. *Farming While Black: Soul Fire Farm's Practical Guide to Liberation on the Land.* Chelsea Green Publishing, 2018.

"Soul Fire Farm: Feeding the Soul, Growing Community." Performance by Leah Penniman, YouTube, *The Laura Flanders Show*, 15 Mar. 2016, www.youtube.com/watch?v=StygQm6YlwQ.

"Farming While Black: Leah Penniman." Performance by Leah Penniman, and Laura Flanders, YouTube, *The Laura Flanders Show*, 8 Dec. 2018, www.youtube.com/watch?v=MYgh7ZFBBQg.

Black Farmers. *USDA*, 2014, pp. 1–2, Black Farmers.

Harrison, Alferdteen. *Black Exodus: the Great Migration from the American South.* Univ. Press of Mississippi, 1992.

Moduloo.net. "Terre De Liens." *Access To Land*, www.accesstoland.eu/-Terre-de-liens-.

"Terre De Liens." *Terre De Liens*, terredeliens.org/.

**What's next**

*Planet on the Mind*

Maniates, Michael and Meyer, John. *The Environmental Politics of Sacrifice*. MIT Press, 2010.

Shiva, Vandana. *Lecture at First Congregational Church*, Berkeley, CA. 11 Feb. 2019.

Washington, Haydn and Cook, John. *Climate Change Denial: Heads In The Sand*, Earthscan, 2011.

www.HowGlobalWarmingWorks.org accessed 17 Jul. 2017.

Ranney, Michael. Personal interview. 14 Jun. 2017.